MAN †UP

BECOMING A GODLY MAN IN AN UNGODLY WORLD

JODY BURKEEN

MAN UP! by Jody Burkeen

© 2011 by Jody Burkeen

Scripture quotations taken from the New American Standard Bible,
Copyright © 1960, 1962, 1963, 1968, 1971, 1972, 1973, 1975, 1977, 1995 by
The Lockman Foundation. Used by permission. (www.Lockman.org)

Editor, Cover Designer, Typesetter: Jeff Gerke
www.wherethemapends.com/publishing_services.html

Library of Congress Cataloging-in-Publication Data
An application to register this book for cataloging has been filed with the Library
of Congress.

International Standard Book Number: 978-0-9839288-1-2

Printed in the United States of America

This book is dedicated to my God-given family.
My wife, Nan, who is drawing closer to the Proverbs 31
woman every day and who is my best friend. Without her, my
life would be meaningless and void. I love you!

My children, two of the most beautiful kids in the world.
Without their miracle births, I may not be the man I am today.

Evee, my daughter, is a tenderhearted, spirited, and beautiful girl. My prayer for her is that she follows God in her every move and never lets anyone influence her otherwise.

Gabe, my son, is a bold, handsome, and God-fearing boy. My prayer for him is that he would become a mighty man of God.

My parents, all of them. I thank you for raising me the way you did, the best you knew how. I love you with all my heart.

Michael, Jon, Kellie, and Curtis, my brothers and sister. I would like to thank them for the many wonderful years of growing up together. Lots of fond memories.

Acknowledgments

I want to thank my Lord and Savior, Jesus Christ, for saving me from my own destruction. I thank Him for giving me the words that are on these pages.

A special thanks to my brother Jon. Without him and his diligence to the Word and his always truthful comments, this book would have taken a lot longer. I want to thank him for writing and rewriting the 30-day challenge with me.

Thanks to all the men who have been a big part of my life and a big part of this book. Keith M.: If it weren't for you, I may not have liked church at all. You were a big part of my spiritual growth, and I miss our days at Denny's.

Dave C., Dennis N., and Ron H.: Thank you, guys, for sitting in on two years of Monday morning Bible studies. It has been awesome.

David L., Dan F., and Del F.: Thank you, all, for your encouragement and accountability. It keeps me straight.

Gary S: Thank you for the encouragement and for keeping my finances straight.

Russell P: Thanks for all those days in the office when we could bounce things off of each other.

Lastly, to all those who read this book: I pray it helps you become a man of God and that you spend the rest of your life trying to *Man Up!* God's way.

TABLE OF CONTENTS

INTRODUCTION

Think back to your childhood. Most every man will be able to recall the time when he was growing from a boy to a man. The title of this book comes from that point in childhood when you were trying to assert yourself into manhood, a time when you had to *man up*.

Perhaps you can remember a time when you were called a sissy. It might have been from the school bully, your best friend, or even your father, but you remember it vividly. "Sissy," they said, dogging you about some situation you were in.

It might have been sports, a fight, or even just a jump over the creek. Someone challenged you by calling you a sissy. At that moment, you had a choice: you could walk away and continue to be a sissy in the eyes of the accuser, or you could puff your chest out, grab your "webbles," and take the challenge. All of us walked away at least once. It's painful, I know, but I'd like you to remember that day, that one moment in time when you were a coward by someone's reckoning.

No matter how insignificant the situation, I'm guessing that part of you still feels like a coward today for turning down the challenge.

Maybe you can also recall a time when you stood up to the challenge. But this memory is more about accomplishment or victory, not failure. It's a memory of that day you were no longer a sissy.

But now you are a grown man. The days of childhood bullies and peer pressure are behind you.

Or are they?

Although there aren't many people calling you a sissy to your face, it may be that you're unknowingly acting like one. Take a look at what the Apostle Paul wrote in the Bible:

> And do not be conformed to this world, but be transformed
> by the renewing of your mind, so that you may prove what
> the will of God is, that which is good and acceptable and
> perfect. (Romans 12:2)

You may actually be allowing the world to dictate how you live, how you act, and how you don't act as a Christian man. If you are doing this, you are, in essence, a "spiritual sissy" because you are walking away from the challenge Jesus has laid out before you in the Bible.

> And He summoned the crowd with His disciples, and said
> to them, "If anyone wishes to come after Me, he must deny
> himself, and take up his cross and follow Me. For whoever
> wishes to save his life will lose it, but whoever loses his life
> for My sake and the gospel's will save it." (Mark 8:34–35)

It's a challenge that is requiring you to take a stand for God's kingdom, not the kingdom of the world, and TO be prepared for the "bullies" of the world to hate you as they hated

Jesus. It's a choice to be a sissy or not to be a sissy, to *ManUp!* or shut up. It's a choice to be different from the world. It's the choice to be an intentional Christian.

Some of the biggest spiritual sissies are in the church today! This book is written with a concerned heart for the Christian man. He is being pulled in a million directions and losing the battle. It's time to man up and get serious about saving the modern-day Christian man—before we become extinct.

Are you or other men you know having trouble in their Christian walk? Do you want to make a difference for God's kingdom? It is my prayer and my hope that this book will open your eyes to the trouble that Christian men are in today. The good news is that these are troubles that can be avoided if we will just *Man Up* and follow Jesus. Join me on a journey through seven areas in a Christian man's life that need major attention. Areas in which we can add some spiritual muscle and stop being 98-pound spiritual weaklings.

In a minute you will read my testimony, and there you will see the 98-pound spiritual weakling I am referring to. It will give you a glimpse of the struggles I faced and the spiritual workout I used to gain the spiritual muscle I need to face life's challenges. The courage comes from Him: "I can do all things through Him who strengthens me" (Philippians 4:13).

Jesus changed me, and that changed my family. And *that* enhanced my witness for Christ and allowed me to be the man He's called me to be. My hope is that someday it will change the world. Join me in this hope.

WORKBOOK INTRODUCTION

These workbook sections include questions for you to answer by yourself or in discussion with other men.

1. In your own words define "spiritual ~~sissy~~." *sus*
2. Do you live in the world (Matthew 13:22, Matthew 16:26, Colossians 2:8) or of the world (Romans 12:2, 1 John 2:15)? Explain what you mean.
3. There is no biblical definition for "spiritual sissy," but how do you think the Bible would describe someone who is skirting his God-given responsibilities?
4. Has there ever been a time in your life when someone challenged you to stop being a spiritual sissy? How did you respond? Minister to Jessie
5. What's one thing you can do this week to stop being a spiritual sissy?
6. Who can I share this book with?

This Week's Challenge: Let God rule your life—because you *can't.*

A SISSY'S TESTIMONY

When I was a young boy, my mom did the best she could in raising me. I was the oldest of five and a member of a family dealing with divorce. My mom and dad had divorced when I was four, and she had been left to raise three kids all by herself.

I had just turned seven when Mom remarried. My brother and sister and I were welcomed into a new family by my stepfather. He added my stepbrother to our family. A few years later, my father married my stepmom. Within ten months, I had a half-brother. In total, there were five of us. I then had three brothers and a sister.

During my early years, my mother and stepfather were very devout in going to church. I always tell people that by the age of twelve I had a drug addiction—I was *drug* to church every time the doors were open. This was where I learned about the Bible and also where I learned to hate the church. By the time I was thirteen, I hated church so much I was causing problems at home just so I didn't have to go.

My hatred stemmed from many reasons, but it came mostly because I began to see the hypocrisy of the church. People saying one thing in the church and doing something different outside of it. I just couldn't take fake people. So this was my opportunity to separate myself from the church. It was also an opportunity for me to be overtaken by the world. My early years in church were spent with people telling me the rules and regulations, but never why I would go to hell if I didn't follow them. Never once was I shown how to have a relationship with Christ.

But in my justification of my hatred of religion and the hypocrisy behind it, I was just being a coward. Too scared to search for myself for the real meaning of Christianity. Deep down inside, I was a sissy.

For the next few years, I lived with my dad and stepmom. I just couldn't handle living with my mom and stepdad, who always made me feel guilty about church. Living with my dad and stepmom was like moving to another planet. It was completely void of guilt or shame about church. I think both of them were a lot like me in that for them church had just become a religion and not a relationship. I now had a freedom that I had never had before: freedom to express myself, to say what I wanted to say, and to do whatever I wanted to do. This is when I began to hate everything to do with God, the church, and everyone involved with church.

Although all four of my parents were great parents, throughout my life there were times they were there for me and times they were not. There were times they lifted me up and times they let me down, and vice versa. This book is not about how I was raised, but more about how the choices I made though my life were a part of God's sovereign master plan.

High School

By the time I finished high school, my disdain for church and the people who went to church grew more and more. For some reason I became angry at God (assuming there even was one) and even more angry at the church.

I had started drinking heavily, and now I began to do drugs. My weekends were spent looking for trouble, and most times I found it. I remember spending one summer with a group of guys who made me look like a choir boy. Just about every weekend we were fighting, stealing, and chasing everything and everybody we could.

One night we broke into a house, and I was the getaway driver. We took a safe out of the house and put it into a four-door car. This safe weighed as much as the car, but somehow we managed to get it into the back seat. As we drove through town to take the safe somewhere so we could cut it open, we pulled next to a police car at a stop light.

Here we were, four big guys in the front seat of a car and a safe in the back, stopped at a stop light waiting for it to turn green. To this day, I don't know why the cop never looked our way, but he kept his eyes straight and drove on through the light. We then drove to a garage to break open the safe . . . and to clean our underwear.

That summer night was the last time I ever stole a thing. I was scared straight by that encounter. In case you're wondering, we did break into that safe, only to find four rolls of quarters and an old handgun. I could have spent years in jail for forty dollars and a broken gun.

Marriage

In 1988 I met my beautiful wife. We began dating in college and married in August of 1990. I was twenty-one and she had just turned twenty-two. Our wedding was very simple, and our honeymoon was spent traveling to my duty station at Fort Riley, Kansas. I had just finished Army boot camp, and we were privileged enough to get to start our lives together in Fort Riley.

After a few years of marriage, my wife began to think twice about what she had gotten herself into. I was a handful. I was a lazy slob, and I didn't really have a care in the world. I pretty much allowed my wife to raise me as her child. Not really being her husband, especially in the biblical sense. She was the head of the household, and I liked it. For me, there was no responsibility, no failure, and no success. I just coasted along in our marriage. It was great—for a season. Unfortunately, this season went on for eleven years.

Money

"You shall have no other gods before Me" (Exodus 20:3).

About eight years into my marriage, I began to get serious about creating wealth. I had finally found a god I could worship: money.

It was awesome. At one point I thought about changing my last name to Jones, because everyone was trying to keep up with me (you'll get that later). My house, my cars, and all my worldly stuff was the best and the most expensive. I was a complete showoff. And I loved it! I remember people trying to witness to me, especially family, and I would tell them "Just look at my stuff—whose god loves them more?" What a jerk I was.

I was headed to the top, and nothing was going to stop me. I have always gotten what I wanted, and right then I wanted more. In 1998, I started buying real estate. This was how I was going to be rich. My wife and I bought two houses and ten condos within a year. Our portfolio was looking good. Donald Trump, look out, here I come.

Money had become my god, and I was worshiping it daily. In my mind, it was the lifeblood I needed to make me feel important and that I had arrived. My god was taking care of me . . . for now.

Kids

After eleven years of marriage, my wife and I wanted to have kids. We were ready, and, so, like everything else, I was going to get what I wanted.

But that didn't happen. I found out, after many months of trying, that we weren't able to have kids—and it was me who had the problem. You talk about a punch in the gut. How could I not have kids? I had everything I had ever wanted, and now, when it came to the most natural thing on earth to do, I couldn't do it! I was hacked off. As a matter of fact, I cursed God. I asked Him, "Of all things, why take away this? Not a good way of getting me to believe in You."

After a few months of feeling sorry for myself, my wife and I tried in-vitro fertilization. Two times. Once again, it failed, and we were disappointed. I cursed God again. And, after much anger and heartbreak thinking I had failed as a man, we came to what would become a wonderful conclusion: We should adopt.

The Miracle

My wife was a pharmaceutical sales representative, so she had many contacts in the medical world. She began to put out feelers for a good adoption agency we could use or even if anyone knew of someone who had a child for adoption. After a few weeks of talking about it to numerous doctors and nurses, she ran across a nurse who had a friend with a daughter who was pregnant and looking into adoption.

My wife rushed home and told me the news, and we were prepared to call her that night. We were excited but not overly optimistic. Well, that night came, and the nurse called us and told us the young girl had run away. Another blow to my emotions. Once again, I turned my anger to God.

A few months later, when my wife was making her usual sales calls, she stopped back by the doctor's office where the nurse worked who knew the girl who had run away. She hesitantly stopped by just to say "hi" to the nurse because the thought of opening up old wounds seemed too hard to bear. But after a polite greeting and some niceties, the nurse told my wife that she hadn't heard from the pregnant girl. My wife left a little disheartened and went on her way.

Miraculously, that night, we received a call from the nurse enthusiastically telling us they'd found the girl and that she wanted to talk with us. We freaked! We were excited and nervous, fumbling with what to say to this girl.

By this time she was seven months pregnant. A few days after our conversation, we went to the house of the girls' parents and met with her. Our meeting was awkward and very intense, but all went well. She liked us, and we fell in love with her. So we began the process of adoption.

Fast-forward to two months later. I was sitting in the hospital praying to a God I didn't believe in, waiting for the birth of a child that I hoped would become my daughter. My wife had the privilege to be in the birthing room and was able to witness the beautiful birth of our daughter.

Once the doctors had checked her and the nurses had cleaned her, they handed her to my wife. She then came to me, overflowing with joy. We couldn't believe we were staring at our daughter.

Months later, life was back to normal. The adoption was final, work was busy, and I was back to building my empire. My wife was back to work, and we hired a full time nanny to take care of our daughter. Life was great! Once again, I had gotten everything I had ever wanted and didn't need anyone's help to do it . . . so I thought.

Later that year, my wife and I moved to a new state. We wanted to leave behind all that was in our past. Starting a new life, we built a new house and were ready to conquer our new jobs.

Within a few weeks of moving, the same young girl called us. As my wife was talking with her, I saw her eyes get wide, and she looked almost scared. Then there were tears welling up in them. My wife covered the phone with her hand and asked me, "How would you like to have a son?"

What? I was jumping off the walls. I was going to have a boy. The young girl was pregnant again, and this time it was going to be a boy.

Once again we had only a couple of months to plan and prepare for another child. We were again blessed to be in the birthing room and again blessed to walk away with a beautiful baby boy. We were overjoyed.

During the birth of both our children, I spent time in the waiting rooms praying to God. This was the first time I ever remember praying. I prayed at both births: "God, if You're real, please bring this child into this world healthy, make the child mine, and I will do whatever You want." Each time, God gave me what I asked for, and each time I broke my promise, the promise to do whatever He wanted.

After the births, life began to become normal. Back to work, a live-in nanny, and the world was ours to conquer. Life was good. Nowhere in my life was a resemblance of any promise I had made to God. I was back in the "world," and that was all that mattered.

The Change

Having children changes your life. For me, I drank and partied less. For my wife, she couldn't stand the thought of someone else raising her children and often thought of staying home. This was when she and I started to struggle.

My fear was that there was no way we could maintain our current lifestyle if my wife quit her job. I loved the life we were living, even though it was tearing our family apart. I didn't think I could make it without the money. So I basically told my wife she didn't have a choice—she had to work.

When my kids were one and two, my wife came to me and reminded me of a promise I had made early in our marriage. The promise was that I would take my kids to church when they were old enough. What she didn't realize was that in that promise there had been a catch. In my mind I wanted to take the kids to church so they could learn to hate church as badly as I did. Then we would never have to go again! But she didn't know about the catch. In her mind, it was a chance for us to be a complete family.

The Church

So, one Sunday morning, for the first time since the kids were born, we went to church. I'll never forget it. We were driving down the street, and I turned to my wife. "Which church are we going to?" At this point in our marriage, she was still very much head of the household. She made the plans, and I just showed up.

But she wouldn't tell me where we were going. In my mind, I had my vision of church and what it should be like. And there was nothing like that in the town we were living.

When we reached a certain spot on the road, she had me pull into a hotel parking lot. "Park here."

"Where!" I asked.

"Here, in the hotel parking lot," she said. "The church is here."

I scoffed. "No way am I going to a church in a hotel."

The materialistic, self-conscious, showoff side of me was coming out. My thought of a church was that it should at least be in its own building. A *church*. Not a hotel. At this point, I was pretty much cussing her and refusing to go in. But she reminded me of the promise to take my kids to church. So, like a little kid pouting, I went in. I was reminded of my early childhood drug problem. Once again I was being *drug* into church.

I grabbed the kids and walked madly into to the old Holidome. "If they want us to sell flowers at the airport," I murmured to my wife, "we are out of here."

Well, come to find out, it wasn't a cult. It was a church full of loving, non-hypocritical sinners. They took us in with open arms. It was nothing like the church I remembered growing up in.

I couldn't get enough.

Filling the Hole

For most of my teenage and adult life, I was an addict of just about anything that was addictive. From pornography to drinking, to drugs and even to sports, I was addicted. Throughout all stages of my life, I had some form of addiction.

X-rated videos and Internet pornography grabbed hold of my life, and I brought it into the bedroom, coaxing my wife to believe we needed it. In my social life, I became a drunk. I was the guy who was the life of the party—'til the party was over. I didn't know how to drink socially, only to be a social drunk. Alcohol had become a part of my social life, and I thought I couldn't live without it.

But once I began going to church, my family and I never missed a time the doors were open. Sunday school, Sunday worship, Sunday night and Wednesday night devotions—we were there. There was a hole of emptiness in my soul, and all the drugs, drinking, pornography, and money I was stuffing into that proverbial hole didn't satisfy me. But now I had finally found something that was satisfying. That something was Jesus Christ.

Salvation

After months of hearing God's Word on a constant basis at this church, it slowly deprogrammed my worldly brain. God began to penetrate my hardened heart, and changes started happening.

On May 21, 2003, my wife and I invited our pastor over to our house. We spent hours praying and talking with the pastor. I had a few questions left unanswered, mostly about the church, the leadership, and the direction of the church. These weren't really critical questions, per se, but, I think, looking back on it, that they were just a distraction from the inevitable: my salvation.

Feeling the prompting of the Holy Spirit, my wife and I gave our lives to Christ that night.

If you confess with your mouth Jesus as Lord and believe in your heart that God raised Him from the dead, you will be saved; for with the heart a person believes, resulting in righteousness, and with the mouth he confesses, resulting in salvation. (Romans 10:9–10)

I can't explain the feeling I had that night. Maybe it felt like accomplishment. I had finally kept the promises I'd made to God when my kids were being born. I had finally given my life to Him and had begun the process of doing His will for my life.

Whatever the feeling, I knew things were going to be different. I just never knew how much so. The process of becoming what I am now is what this book is about. It's a process that involves God, my family, and the church. It's a process that isn't easy and is not for the lukewarm. I knew I had to *Man Up*.

But God never said that following Him would be easy. Look at what Jesus says in Matthew 10:34–39:

> "Do not think that I came to bring peace on the earth; I did not come to bring peace, but a sword. For I came to set a man against his father, and a daughter against her mother, and a daughter-in-law against her mother-in-law; and a man's enemies will be the members of his household. He who loves father or mother more than Me is not worthy of Me; and he who loves son or daughter more than Me is not worthy of Me. And he who does not take his cross and follow after Me is not worthy of Me. He who has found his life will lose it, and he who has lost his life for My sake will find it."

Over the next several chapters, I want to analyze the areas where men need to man up and stop being spiritual sissies. These areas are where I was a sissy and where I am learning to man up every day.

These areas are struggles for all men, and I will be candid as possible about my life and the lives of the men around me. I will be honest and brutal about what it takes and doesn't take to be a Christian man based on God's Word. If we will stop being spiritual sissies, we can man up and change the world. But it can be done only with the help of God.

If you were to study every person used by God in the Bible, you would see that there were a lot of former sissies. But what separated the sissies from the men God used mightily was that moment when the latter chose to allow God to take control of their lives. When they chose to man up.

I pray this book challenges you to do the same. Let God rule your life, and stop being a spiritual sissy. Learn to *Man Up* in faith.

WORKBOOK TESTIMONY

Testimonies are like fingerprints: Each one is different. A testimony can never be argued with or disputed; it's yours and no one else's. It's your proof that Jesus is real in your life. It's true because of the way He changed your life.

So learn to tell your testimony. Even if you don't know a single verse in the Bible, your testimony can be powerful. Write your testimony out, and share it with others. Develop the confidence to have a two-minute, a ten-minute, and forty-five-minute version of your testimony. You never know when or how much time you may have to share it.

> If we receive the testimony of men, the testimony of God is greater; for the testimony of God is this, that He has testified concerning His Son. The one who believes in the Son of God has the testimony in himself; the one who does not believe God has made Him a liar, because he has not believed in the testimony that God has given concerning His Son. And the testimony is this, that God has given us eternal life, and this life is in His Son. He who has the Son has the life; he who does not have the Son of God does not have the life. (1 John 5:9–12)

CHAPTER 1

TIME TO MAN UP PERSONALLY

Now for this very reason also, applying all diligence, in your faith supply moral excellence, and in your moral excellence, knowledge, and in your knowledge, self-control, and in your self-control, perseverance, and in your perseverance, godliness, and in your godliness, brotherly kindness, and in your brotherly kindness, love. For if these qualities are yours and are increasing, they render you neither useless nor unfruitful in the true knowledge of our Lord Jesus Christ. For he who lacks these qualities is blind or short-sighted, having forgotten his purification from his former sins. Therefore, brethren, be all the more diligent to make certain about His calling and choosing you; for as long as you practice these things, you will never stumble; for in this way the entrance into the eternal kingdom of our Lord and Savior Jesus Christ will be abundantly supplied to you. (2 Peter 1:5–11)

IN THE CHURCH TODAY, THERE ARE MEN SITTING in pews and chairs who are as useless as the furniture they are sitting on. Most of them have no clue what they need to do for God's kingdom. Some couldn't care less. Still others are too prideful to step out beyond what they already know and are stuck in their so-called comfort zone.

The church as we know it today is being run by women and a few good men. Women are very important in the church and need to apply their skills where needed. However, most of the men have become complacent, lazy, and disobedient when it comes to spreading the gospel, serving their families, and serving in the church.

The three types of men I described in the paragraph above are easy to spot. First are the men who have no clue what to do or how to do it. These guys are usually new to Christianity. They are green, gung ho, and giddy for Christ. They have a new Bible and are starting to speak "Christianese," but they have very few examples of good, God-fearing men after whom to model their lives. If they are not mentored and discipled soon after salvation, these guys usually fade into the crowd.

Second are the guys who just couldn't care less. These guys are looking to check off Sunday morning church attendance from their to-do list, and they usually feel they are being good Christian men for doing so. No matter what you say or do, they will likely not change unless you can show them there is something in it for them. Their wives have "drugged" them to church. Most of the time they are cordial and sometimes even nice, but they don't want to be involved in anything you have to offer. They are content to wait it out on the back row.

Third are the men who won't change for anything. No matter what you tell them, if it didn't come from the King James Bible, they don't want to hear a word of it. They won't let their guard down for one minute, so their Pharisee-like façade of "I am righteous and holy at all times" stays in place. Although they are usually saved, they are not open to sharing their own past failures and successes to help others in the church. They haven't eliminated their pride and embraced the humility of Christ.

During a Bible study I was teaching a few years back, we were discussing the subject of sexual immorality. I began to talk about the issues I have with my mind and the nasty thoughts that come, primarily through my struggles with pornography. I told the men that I'd always justified it by saying, "It's just in my head—who is it hurting?" But I told them that, as always happens, if you're reading the Bible, God touched you with a verse. That time, it was Matthew 5:27–28:

> "You have heard that it was said, 'You shall not commit adultery'; but I say to you that everyone who looks at a woman with lust for her has already committed adultery with her in his heart."

Jesus was saying that I can't even look at a woman with lust without committing adultery. That is hardcore teaching.

I then turned to the group of men. "What are your struggles with immorality?" I heard many honest answers. It was great. Men opened up, and it seemed like struggles abounded in the group.

But one answer I got shocked me more than any I had heard: "I don't have that kind of problem," a man said, "and I don't think this is a subject that should be talked about in church."

That answer floored me. First, if you are a male and you "have a pair," you've had these thoughts. Second, where else should this be discussed? The church should be the place where we can come together to share one another's burdens and sins.

It became very clear that some men weren't ready to man up. Maybe they never would. I decided I could chalk this one up to the devil. Look what happened: A group of Christian men had been sharing one another's burdens and sins. Then, because of pride the conversation was halted.

Men are falling away from the church because of hypocrisy, because of un-forgiveness, because of continual sin, and because of the lack of accountability. And when men fall, our families fall as well. When the family falls, the community begins to fall, and so forth and so on.

The three groups of men described in this chapter aren't the only kind of men in the church, but they are the most evident. And because of their lukewarm attitude toward Christianity, complacency has become Satan's most powerful tool. Your church may be different. You may have godly men leading and mentoring others. If so, God bless your church. But I feel that the groups of men I described need to be addressed. Especially since they are probably the norm in your church.

We need to change the mindset of the church and learn to be a community full of god-fearing, loving, honest men. Men who take one another under their wings to disciple and mentor. Men who will be bold and will learn to hold each other accountable by the Word of God.

We need to grasp the urgency for change, for us to be intentional in our Christian walk. If we don't change, an entire generation of our children will be in dire straits. But in order to affect these three groups of men, we have to start with ourselves. We have to take 2 Peter 1 to heart and start applying diligence in our faith! The Christian walk takes discipline, and we must be willing to change personally before we can change anyone else.

My hope and prayer for you is that you see the need for radical change in you . . . and the men in your church.

Turning from Being a Spiritual Sissy

Upon salvation in 2003, I began to search the Scriptures as if they had an expiration date. Every day, I was reading and studying to soak in as much information as I possibly could. My goal was to figure out why I hated the church and despised God the way I had before I'd been saved by His grace and become a Christian.

During that search, I found that the Scripture was alive. I mean a breathing, feeling, and *seeing* kind of alive. It was there to console me, enlighten me, and answer all my questions. I began to realize that all my problems and fears could have been eliminated early in my life if someone had explained the Bible to me in a way that I would have understood.

Then it hit me like a ton of bricks: No one had one ever explained to me that Christianity was a relationship, not a religion. My hatred of the church and my anger at God could have been eliminated early in my life if someone would have been bold enough to explain that relationship to me. Now that I am a Christian, I can't allow that to happen to the men I come in contact with.

I had never had a relationship with Jesus. Unfortunately, neither had anyone else in my life. No one could explain to me what it was like or how it felt, because they had never known it themselves. Everyone claimed to know Him and even tried to recite a little Scripture to me.

But it was Scripture that they had heard the preacher use. They had never experienced the life-changing way of the Word of God. It was Scripture that came from the mission statement of the church or the back of the church bulletin or the memory verse they had learned as a child. But it was never from the heart of someone who had felt the transforming love of Christ through Scripture and the Holy Spirit.

I came to the realization that the church as a whole has done a poor job in teaching the meaning of this *relationship* with Jesus. The church is good at teaching religion, but lousy in relationships. I knew then that I had to become disciplined in my studies—and, more importantly, disciplined in the application of the Word to my life. Reading the Scripture daily is the beginning of the relationship we need to have with God. It is His love story that He put in the Bible for us to read.

Through this process of learning to have a relationship with God and allowing the Holy Spirit to change my life, I have lost friends and been ridiculed and judged. But I persevere and boldly accept the challenge God has set before me. I am determined not to be lukewarm in my Christian walk. I am dedicated to becoming a righteous man of God through the reading and application of His Word in my life.

Start with Jesus

If you're tired of being a spiritual sissy, Jesus is the mentor you should start with. Any man who can go forty days without eating is no sissy. But that isn't the only reason we should start with Jesus. The Bible tells us that He is the way and the truth and the life (John 14:6). If we want to get to God, it is through Jesus.

The relationship I was talking about earlier is a relationship with Jesus. You and I have to look to Jesus in order to understand the difference between relationship and religion. Once we have done that, the process of becoming a godly man can begin.

Jesus spent His adult life teaching the difference between religion and relationship. He showed us the difference in the way He spent His spare time. It was spent with God the Father . . . daily. No matter how busy, no matter how dire the situation, Jesus always looked for time to spend with God.

His time spent with God the Father allowed Him to feel comfort in His purpose and to find peace in the knowledge that what He was doing was God's will and not His own. Could Jesus have known His purpose without praying? Or could He have found peace without praying? Of course He could've, He was God. But when God gave us His Son as our example for life, He needed to show us the best way to spend time with the Father, and that was through prayer.

Do you know without a shadow of a doubt that you are in God's will? Do you have peace like a river? If not, how much time are you spending with God the Father through Jesus the Son? Minutes, hours, days? This time spent with the Father will ultimately keep you from being a spiritual sissy. In order for us to effect change in our lives, our families, our church, and the world, we must become godly men seeking a relationship with Jesus.

The time spent with Him will dictate how godly you become. The time spent with Jesus will also dictate how the rest of your life falls into place. Not that being in God's will is easy or that it's a magic formula to a happy life. But this time in prayer will give you strength when you are in trials, humbleness when you are prideful, forgiveness when you want revenge, and love when you want to hate. This time with Jesus will begin to affect the rest of your life for the better. It starts with you and God through Jesus Christ.

This personal time will then affect your marriage, which will in turn affect your family, which will in turn affect your church, which will in turn affect the world.

God is looking for godly, manly men to make a difference for His kingdom, and you cannot just sit back and wait for someone else to do it. Let's stop being spiritual sissies and embrace the challenge. God is not looking for someone who can chew steel and bend iron, but for a man who will serve others, pray with his wife, read the Word to his kids, and be a godly example to those around him.

Begin by kneeling. Then pray and listen. God will lead you away from being a spiritual sissy when you seek His face. "Call to Me and I will answer you, and I will tell you great and mighty things, which you do not know" (Jeremiah 33:3).

Discipline

In 1990, I was tired of college, and I started falling behind in my studies. I felt as if there were no way out of the hole I was in unless I started all over, and I wasn't about to do that. One night while on a date with the woman who is now my wife, we watched the Clint Eastwood movie *Heartbreak Ridge*. For some reason, that movie impacted me. So much so that the next day I went and joined the army. No kidding, one day after seeing that movie I dropped out of school and joined the army.

Two months later I was at Fort Knox, Kentucky, reporting for boot camp. (Disclaimer—as a Christian man now, I do not recommend you watch the movie *Heartbreak Ridge*. It's not something I think Jesus would watch with you.)

I had played football most of my life and was pretty muscular, but during college I'd started drinking and drugging pretty heavily, so all my muscle had turned to fat. When I got off the bus to report to my barracks, the drill sergeant spotted me a mile away. As he barreled through 160 other guys to get to me, I knew I was in trouble.

When he finally got to me, we were nose to nose. The brim of his hat was sitting on top of my head. He looked me dead in the eyes and said, "You're going to be my project this semester, fat boy!" In essence he was calling me a sissy and daring me to man up to the challenge. I knew I was dead meat for the next sixteen weeks. But I was ready for the challenge.

In boot camp, there were many milestones that we had to pass in order to move to the next level. Hand-to-hand combat, physical fitness, and marksmanship were each challenges in and of themselves.

In our first week, the army gave us a rubber M16 rifle. The rubber weapon was used to teach us how to hold, carry, and store our M16. They didn't trust us with the real one just yet, so we trained with the fake.

Over the next few weeks, after learning how to hold and respect the rubber M16, we got a real M16, but it had a lock on the barrel. Our drill sergeants still weren't ready to trust us. After a few more days we were allowed to take the lock off and use an empty magazine cartridge. It started to feel a little more like the real thing, but it was still not able to inflict damage.

At last came the moment of truth: the firing range. We had finally earned the trust to use our weapons. We were given a full metal jacket—real bullets. This was it: a gun, bullets, and a target to shoot.

As I aimed my weapon downfield and pulled the trigger, I finally understood the power of the weapon I had in my hand. It could save lives, and it could take lives. I was given the power to protect and serve my country. In that sense, this weapon could save lives. But on the battlefield, it would take a life with one shot. That is a lot of power and responsibility.

It took discipline to get to the point of being able to use an M16: weeks of grueling drills and training. But it all had a purpose in the end. That purpose was to have us understand the power that we actually had when holding a fully loaded M16 in our hands.

The Bible has the same power. But as long as it's closed, it's like the rubber M16 I carried. You can learn to hold it, you can store it, but if it stays closed, you can never use it. If you open your Bible, it starts to become real, much like the M16 with the lock. An open Bible begins to look real but still isn't capable of much power. But as you start to read the words on the page, the Bible becomes much like the M16 with an empty magazine. Everything is working but it still doesn't have the power or the bullets to save or take lives.

But then, as you apply to your life what the Word says, you become an M16 with a full metal jacket. James 1:22 says, "But prove yourselves doers of the word, and not merely hearers who delude themselves." It's now time to aim, pull the trigger, and be ready to share the good news of Christ.

Someone was brave enough to share it with you—with whom are you going to share it? Now you have the power to change lives, to save lives, and sometimes the power to take a life from the grasp of the enemy, that being the lives of those who are in the hold of Satan.

In order to take the lives from the hold of Satan, we have to remove the spiritual fat and add spiritual muscle. In the same way it took discipline in boot camp—where I lost forty pounds of fat and turned it into lean muscles ready for a fight—we have to do the same with the Word of God, only it's a spiritual fight. All this takes discipline.

Are you ready? Are you prepared to begin to use the weapon God has given you? No spiritual sissies are allowed. Like boot camp, this will not be easy. You are God's project now, sissy! He wants you to be a man— godly man for His kingdom and for His will. Are you ready to give up your will and trust His will? It's time to *Man Up* and eliminate pride, embrace humility, and surrender to our Lord Jesus Christ. This will take discipline, and it will take God's help. You and I cannot do this alone.

"And looking at them Jesus said to them, 'With people this is impossible, but with God all things are possible'" (Matthew 19:26).

How To Begin the Relationship
"He must increase, but I must decrease" (John 3:30 30).

This is where you and I need to get out of the way. With us in the way, God's will cannot be done, and we will continue to be spiritual sissies.

In order for God to finish the good work He started in us, we must repent of the sins that hinder us from being used by God. You should fall on your knees and beg God to forgive you of the sins that are currently in your life. "If we confess our sins, He is faithful and righteous to forgive us our sins and to cleanse us from all unrighteousness" (1 John 1:9).

To begin the process of learning to *Man Up,* we need to start with a heart transplant. Not literally, but spiritually. We begin by asking God to cleanse us, forgive us, and renew us to be the new creation we became at salvation (2 Corinthians 5:17).

Before you go any further, stop right now and ask God to forgive you.

With that behind you, His will can be done. Insert the date of your forgiveness here _9/21/14_. With this clean start, the slate is clean in order for God to begin making the changes needed in your life.

Read Your Bible

If you have been a Christian for any extended period of time, you have heard people tell you to read your Bible. You might even have heard Joshua 1:8:

> "This book of the law shall not depart from your mouth, but you shall meditate on it day and night, so that you may be careful to do according to all that is written in it; for then you will make your way prosperous, and then you will have success."

So why is it so hard to read it? Because, like most new things, we don't know how. Most of us start in Genesis and try to work our way to Revelation. We start off fast and furious, but by the time we hit Numbers and Deuteronomy, we are spent. We don't get to share in the power of God's Word because we don't allow it to soak in. So we quit.

It's much like exercise. After a few weeks of sweating we start to get discouraged when we don't see the results. But if we would keep going, the change would be noticeable in the way we look and feel. Reading the Bible is the same way—we have to stick to it in order to see the results.

In 2004, I began reading my Bible every day. My goal was to finish it all the way through. It didn't take me long, once I put my mind to it. Through the process of reading it, I started to see changes in my life, and so did others.

The Word of God began to take over my life in ways I wasn't expecting. I began to become a better husband. I took over the role as the spiritual head of the household. I became a better father by raising my kids by the Bible and not just by my own beliefs. I became a better member at my church. I learned to serve and not just sit. I became a better businessman, and I started running our company for God instead of myself. Slowly but surely, God was changing me from the inside out.

Make it a habit to read your Bible every day. Someone once said, "Don't eat physically until you eat spiritually." I have made that a part of my life. You can't use the Word in your life unless you read it.

There are a ton of books on how to read your Bible. I would suggest that you start by reading it chronologically, in the order the events happened in history. This allows you to read it in a smooth, flowing context based on the events as they occurred in real time. It might help you understand the rhyme and reason of the Bible. If this method doesn't work for you, find one that does. No matter what method you use, just read your Bible.

Once you have become consistent in your Bible reading, start a Bible *study*. Not with a group but on your own. Read through the Scripture, small segments at a time. Get a dictionary, a concordance, and a commentary, and start really digging into Scripture to find out more about the history, the authors, and the people God used to tell His story. By doing this, you will gain a better appreciation for the words that are written on the page. (See the study method described at the end of this book.)

Once you have started to feel the words God has written, start imparting them to others. Allow God's words to work through you to impact someone else's life.

And don't stop reading. There is never an ending point to Scripture. Once you think you have it all figured out, you will see something in the Word that you have never seen before. You may have read it a thousand times, but never that Scripture in that way. The Word never changes, but we do. We have seasons in our life that allows the Word to pierce us differently than the last time we read it.

Start by repenting of your sins. Begin reading your Bible every day, and don't stop reading. Then pray.

Man Up and Pray

"Pray without ceasing" (1 Thessalonians 5:17).

If you can learn anything from Jesus, it's how to pray. We seem to take this for granted. Which means we are real spiritual sissies when it comes to prayer. Oh, we are very good at the popcorn prayers: "Dear Lord, help me with . . . " or "Lord, can You . . . " But we don't take time to really get in touch with God through prayer. To have a heartfelt conversation with God is something lukewarm Christians have a hard time doing. Pride, sin, or laziness keeps us from truly communicating with God, and yet this is where we need the discipline the most.

The twelve apostles saw Jesus do miracles, preach great sermons, and stump some of the greatest minds of His time. But the one thing they asked Jesus was about prayer: "Lord, teach us how to pray." What? Teach us how to pray? If that had been me, I would have asked Him to teach me to do that cool, walking-on-water thing or raise the dead. What party favorites those would be. But pray? Prayer was so important to Jesus that the apostles saw it—and they obviously saw a change in Him when He did.

Prayer is the connection between us and God. It's our "Batphone" to the Father. The death and resurrection of Jesus Christ gave us the ability to go to God the Father on our own behalf, rather than through priests. And yet most of the time, we waste it. Most of us think prayer is something we do at the dinner table—and then we usually then let our kids say it.

Prayer can help bridge the connection between the reading of Scripture and the applying it to your life. Prayer gives us the chance to talk with the One who will show us the plan for our lives. A prayer life is essential to leaving the world of the spiritual sissies and moving to the world of a Christ-centered manly life.

In 2006, a couple of years into my Christianity, I went to a retreat with a charismatic pastor friend of mine. Before the retreat started, they had the group of pastors come to the theater in order to pray over the retreat and all those who were attending. After a quick hurrah from the featured pastor, we began to pray. I started seeing pastors fall to the ground, lying prostrate, praying to God. Others were on their knees, and others were walking around, but all were praying. At first, I was a little weird-ed out. But once I understood that they didn't care if anyone was watching them and I knew they weren't watching me, I began to pray.

Only a few moments into that prayer, I felt the Holy Spirit come upon me like I had never felt before. I felt as if God were holding me, my head on His shoulder, and He wanted to hear every word I had to say. I had never felt that much peace before. It was amazing.

That day I realized how important prayer was and how much I needed to keep it in my life. It took a moment to let my guard down, but when I did I saw the glory of the Lord. That is how your prayer life should be: Let it all go and pray. You may not start off on your face, but at least start on your knees. Do it while you are alone. It is powerful to be one-on-one with God praying while you are on your knees.

I know you can have an experience like I did. Just abandon all the cares of this world, the thoughts of what "they" think, and pray. Lay all your worries, sins, anxieties, and concerns at the feet of the Almighty. You will feel like you are in the arms of God Himself, just like I did.

I keep a daily journal of my prayers. It is an amazing feeling to read what you prayed about months earlier and see that God did answer your prayer. To be reminded of the little prayer you prayed months earlier and then to see God answer even that little prayer . . . it builds faith. *Man Up* when it comes to prayer. Become a man of heartfelt prayer. To be like Jesus, we need to act like Jesus. He prayed daily. So should we. Man up and get prayed up.

How To Pray

The apostles made this request: "Lord teach us to pray" (Luke 11:1). So Jesus told them how to pray.

This is a great place to start. If you feel you cannot pray or just don't know how, start just like Jesus taught the apostles:

> And He said to them, "When you pray, say: 'Father, hallowed be Your name. Your kingdom come. Give us each day our daily bread. And forgive us our sins, For we ourselves also forgive everyone who is indebted to us. And lead us not into temptation.'" (Luke 11:2)

Then open yourself to whatever takes hold.

The best way to pray is using whatever form of prayer that fits into your life—whatever makes you feel close to God and whatever brings you joy from being with God. It might be two hours of prayer all alone in your office. It might be a two-minute prayer when you remember to. But whatever or however it is, just pray. Pray for others, pray for your family, pray for your church, pray for issues. Pray for all the above, but no matter what, just pray.

Once your prayers become consistent, you will find yourself praying and not even knowing that you're doing it. The Bible tells us to pray without ceasing (1 Thessalonians 5:17). The more you do it, the more you will start praying without ceasing. God wants to hear from us at all times. Use every waking moment that you can to talk with God. Many of the problems you face will be taken care of at the very moment you pray.

God has three ways of answering your prayers: Yes, No, and Wait. Don't get discouraged if God doesn't answer immediately. As a matter of fact, keep praying, and then listen. God will give you an answer when you're ready to receive it.

This is the challenge for you personally. In order for you to become the godly, intentional, Christian man that God has called you to be, start reading your Bible every day, pray every day, and start applying it to your life. Don't be a spiritual sissy, anymore! *Man Up*.

10-19-19

(15 guys)

WORKBOOK CHAPTER 1
TIME TO MAN UP PERSONALLY

1. From the three groups of men in this chapter, which one are you?
   - New to the Christian world?
   - Not really wanting to be in church?
   - So entrenched you're not changing?
   - None of the above. I am striving daily to be the man God has called me to be.

2. Do you have a personal relationship with Jesus? If so, explain what it looks like.

3. Do you even know who He is? Read John 1:1–5 and respond.

4. Are you keeping God from using you because of your sins or unwillingness? If so, explain.

5. How are you getting in God's way (e.g., sin, pride, lack of knowledge)?

6. Read 2 Timothy 3:16–17 and respond.

7. Do you believe the Bible is true? Support your answer.

8. How often are you reading and studying the Bible?

9. Read Philippians 4:6 and 1 Thessalonians 5:17. What do these verses say about praying?

10. How is your prayer life? Describe why you think it's strong or could be stronger.

Memory Verse—John 14:6: "Jesus said to him, 'I am the way, and the truth, and the life; no one comes to the Father but through Me.'"

This Week's Challenge: Read, pray, and apply daily.

CHAPTER 2

MAN UP IN YOUR MARRIAGE

Enjoy life with the woman whom you love all the days of
your fleeting life which He has given to you under the sun;
for this is your reward in life and in your toil in which you
have labored under the sun. (Ecclesiastes 9:9)

AS YOU WALK INTO CHURCHES TODAY, YOU SEE
many of the programs and ministry outreach efforts performed
by . . . women. In some cases, these same women are also the
head of the household, raising kids, paying bills, and sometimes bringing home the bacon. The biblical model that God
gave us—that men should be the leaders in the church and
home—is not being followed by many Christian men today.

Countless married Christian men have become spiritual
sissies. These men have their tail between their legs, and their
wives have them by the collar. Many of these men have allowed
their wives to call all the shots, and they just follow around like
a lost puppy waiting for the next treat. In many cases, it's not
because the wife wants to act this way, but because she doesn't
have the choice: Her husband isn't stepping up.

Don't get me wrong: I am not being a chauvinist with these
statements. Women have a major role to play in God's kingdom and the home, and they are equally gifted in many areas

of ministry. As a matter of fact, the Bible gives us many examples God used mightily for His kingdom. But unfortunately, this has become the stereotypical view of Christian men today: whipped like dogs and too frail to stand up for their God, their family, or their marriage. Men need to bronze themselves and *Man Up.*

The Picture of a Spiritual Sissy Husband

When I was married, in 1990, my wife was far more mature than I ever thought about being. Some might say she still is. But since I became a Christian in 2003, our roles have reversed.

During the first thirteen years of our marriage, my wife was raising me. I mean that in the sense of the way you raise a child. She always had to mold me, scold me, and hold me just like a kid. And I came to the point where I actually liked it. The day before I got married, my mom made my bed. The day after I got married, my wife made it. I had just gone from one mom to the other. I was the biggest sissy around. My wife was my mom, not my soul-mate. She spent many years training me to become a man. It didn't work too well because that isn't the biblical model, and I think over time she finally stopped trying and just let go.

In the early years of our marriage, when people asked us about having kids, I would jokingly say, "She has to raise me first." What I later realized was that it wasn't a joke. Not a good way to be a biblical husband.

> Husbands, love your wives, just as Christ loved the church
> and gave himself up for her to make her holy, cleansing her
> by the washing with water through the word, and to present
> her to himself as a radiant church, without stain or wrinkle

we have a responsibility

or any other blemish, but holy and blameless. In this same way, husbands ought to love their wives as their own bodies. He who loves his wife loves himself. After all, no one ever hated his own body, but he feeds and cares for it, just as Christ does the church—for we are members of his body. "For this reason a man will leave his father and mother and be united to his wife, and the two will become one flesh." (Ephesians 5:25–31)

After I accepted Jesus as my Lord and Savior, I began to read what the Bible says about being a good Christian husband. What I found was that I wasn't even close to the biblical model, and neither were most of the men I'd met in church.

But reading about what kind of husband I needed to be and actually doing it were two different things. I had thirteen years of bad habits to get rid of. An old, comfortable routine. I had a wife to convince that I had changed, and I had to close my ears to Satan telling me I couldn't do it. This so far has been the biggest challenge for me in my Christian walk.

In my marriage, I had made a lot of mistakes. I had let my wife down more than once. So for me to start trying to assert my newfound "spiritual head of the household" attitude . . . well, it was going to take a long time, a lot of prayer, and actions that were much different than what I had shown in the past. As she has always said, "Actions speak louder than words."

My wife had spent our marriage providing the majority of the income. She had moved up in the ranks as a pharmaceutical saleswoman in the largest company in the industry. She was successful, beautiful, and confident, and she was fast becoming the number one salesperson in the company. This was something I was proud of but also very jealous of. The jealously part is something I didn't bring up very often.

But after having kids, my wife's job began to suffer. We had a full-time live-in nanny while we both worked, but the thought of leaving her children with another woman became just too painful and began to affect her attitude at work.

On top of all this, for the first time in our lives, we were listening to the Holy Spirit and allowing Him to direct our lives. What He was telling us to do was a hard pill for me to swallow. God was telling my wife she needed to stay at home with our kids.

This was not something I felt like we needed to do. Not because God wasn't talking to me too, but because I was not ready for this kind of change. All I was worried about was the money, the lifestyle, and having to step up and be the man of the house.

If God is calling you to do something, no matter how far-fetched, He will see you through it. It won't be without trial or without error, but He will see you through to the end.

> Consider it all joy, my brethren, when you encounter various trials knowing that the testing of your faith produces endurance. And let endurance have its perfect result, so that you may be perfect and complete, lacking in nothing. (James 1:2–4)

God Spoke

After fighting through the conflict and after I was eventually convicted by God that my wife did need to stay home with the kids, she quit her job, and we haven't looked back since.

Although there have been trials and tribulations in our life, it was the best thing we have done to date. As I said earlier, God will get you through the bad times if He called you to it.

Look at Paul. After God called Him on the road to Damascus, he spent many years in prison, faced death and stoning, and was shipwrecked. But he followed God's call, and this is what he said near the end of his life: "I have fought the good fight, I have finished the course, I have kept the faith" (2 Timothy 4:7).

God's plan for your life may not turn out as you want it to, but whose plan would you rather live—yours or His? Keep fighting the good fight.

After listening to God, my wife quit her job to stay home, and God began to do a mighty work in both of us. For my wife, it was to start letting me take over as head of the household, both spiritually and financially. For me, it was to become the man God intended me to be. We both dug into Scripture to figure out what it was we were to do. Through this process we have had ups and downs, but, thus far, God has been faithful to us.

Listening to God and My Wife

My wife tells me that my ears have a certain frequency that they're deaf to and that her voice must be in the range I can't hear, because most of the time when she is talking I'm not listening.

For me, and I think for most men, listening is an acquired trait. We don't do it easily, and for us it is work. But in a marriage and with God, there has to be listening.

Men are prone to act, not listen. We want to fix things before we even know the complete story. I know that many times while my wife is talking I am already fixing her or her situation. But usually she just needs me to listen. I thank God that He is teaching me this daily. I believe that only through prayer and the Word would I have ever learned this important fact. We need to listen more—and not only listen but hear, as well.

The following statement is not based on any poll or scientific study, but is merely a gut feeling: if Christian men would stand up and fight for their marriages, listen to their wives, and be the Christian men God intends them to be, divorce in the church would come to a screeching halt. But until a revival begins in the heart of men and in our churches, it's our duty, mine and yours, to *Man Up* in our marriage. Begin by simply listening. *Give yourself up*

Love Your Wife As . . .

"Husbands, love your wives, just as Christ loved the church and gave himself up for her to make her holy, cleansing her by the washing with water through the word" (Ephesians 5:25–26).

Imagine if you and I really loved our wives as Christ loved the church. Our marriages would be unstoppable. Let me ask you this question: Have you tried to love your wife like Christ loves the church?

The verse above tells us that we should make her holy and cleanse her with the word. What does that mean? One thing it means is that if we will start with praying for our wives, speaking the Word of God over our wives, and reading the Word of God with our wives, we will be on the way to loving her like Christ loved the church.

Men have forgotten what it means to be a gentleman. In the age of "it's all about me" we forget that it's really not about us. It's about our wives and kids. We need to be sacrificial when it comes to our spouses. We need to give up the weekend golf outing when she needs a break. We need to open the car door when we are out with her. And we need to talk with her instead of watching TV.

These are very simple ways we can start loving our wives. You'll be amazed at the impact these small little steps will make in your marriage.

Start simply by doing the things mentioned above or something you don't normally do or are normally in trouble for not doing. These things will go a long way with your wife.

A Praying Husband

If you were to think of the Bible as the brain of Christianity, prayer would be the heart. This is where the body gets the life-sustaining blood to keep the body going.

In our Christian walk as well as in our own bodies, we need the brain and the heart, the Bible and the prayer. But since prayer comes from the heart, many men fail to pray at all and certainly not with their wives. In most cases, our actions are a reflection of our prayer life and the reflection of our heart. If you're not in the Word and praying on a daily basis personally, it is hard to pray with your wife. Besides God, your wife knows what's inside of you more than anyone. She knows if you're a hypocrite in your walk, and that makes you shy away from praying with her.

I remember the first time I tried to pray with my wife. It started off with the typical request, "Lord, please bless our family. Bless our marriage. Thank You for this and thank You for that." I then began to get out of my comfort zone. I started praying for others to be better in their walk. I mentioned friends and family who I knew weren't living the lives of intentional

Christians. I started to get a bad feeling as I was praying—because I knew that what I was praying for others to do was something I wasn't doing myself. I stopped and looked at my wife, knowing she thought I was a hypocrite.

She never said a word, but she didn't have to. I knew I was a hypocrite. So from that moment on, I made a promise to God to do whatever it took to make sure I wasn't that guy anymore. And this time, it wasn't like the promises I'd made in hospital waiting rooms. I didn't forget these.

In order for your marriage to last in this evil world we live in, you need to be in prayer for and with your wife. And now more than ever. With the divorce rate as high in the church as it is outside of the church, it's time we did something different.

As you begin to make strides in your personal relationship with Christ, it will filter into your marriage. Trust me—I saw it work firsthand in my marriage.

Are you listening to your wife? Are you praying for and with your wife? If not, you will never be the husband God intended you to be.

You Start First

Albert Einstein was quoted saying, "Insanity is doing the same thing over and over again and expecting different results." I see men in the church trying to strong-arm their wives into submitting to them. Over and over again I hear them say, "I'll change when she changes," but to no avail. Their marriage is stuck in the vicious cycle of insanity.

The cycle of insanity can be easily broken by taking Ephesians 5 to heart. Unfortunately, when men read Ephesians the only verse we tend to read is Ephesians 5:22: "Wives, be subject to your husbands." We fail to see the following verses, which challenge us to be like Christ, not some overbearing brute who bullies our wives with the Bible.

But guess what: it's a two-way street. A contract. If we do not love our wives as Christ loved the church, then our wives don't have to be subject to us. Let me put it this way: If you want your wife to be subject to you (but not as your slave), you first must give yourself up for her, just like Christ did for the church. That means we start first. *Man Up* and stop the cycle of insanity.

Imagine if Christ had waited for the church to get right before He gave Himself up for it. If He'd done that, we would still be waiting for our Savior.

You go first. You don't wait for her to do something before you do your part. Your wife needs to see the change in you first. And then, over time, you will begin to show her that you love her as Christ loves the church. She will see that you are willing to lay down your life for her. At that time, she will begin to submit to you, because she knows without a shadow of a doubt that you are in a right relationship with Christ. Then and only then will she submit.

One of the best explanations I have found on the meaning of "submission" is from the website www.gotquestions.org:

> Submission is a natural response to loving leadership. When a husband loves his wife as Christ loves the church (Ephesians 5:25–33), then submission is a natural response from a wife to her husband. The Greek word translated "submit," *hupotasso,* is the continuing form of the verb. This means that submitting to God, the government, or a husband is not a one-time act. It is a continual attitude, which becomes a pattern of behavior. The submission talked about

in Ephesians 5 is not a one-sided subjection of a believer to a selfish, domineering person. Biblical submission is designed to be between two Spirit-filled believers who are mutually yielded to each other and to God. Submission is a two-way street. Submission is a position of honor and completeness. When a wife is loved as the church is loved by Christ, submission is not difficult. Ephesians 5:24 says, "Now as the church submits to Christ, so also wives should submit to their husbands in everything." This verse is saying that the wife is to submit to her husband in everything that is right and lawful. Therefore, the wife is under no obligation to disobey the law or God in the name of submission. (www.gotquestions.org/wives-submit.html, accessed 11/01/2010)

So, let's stop being spiritual sissies in our marriages. Let's get on our knees and pray for our wives. Let's pray that God shows us how to be like Christ and how to give ourselves up to our wives. Then let's pray with our wives. This may be the hardest thing to do because she knows you like no one else. But let the Spirit take over and be honest in your prayers. Then read the Word of God with her any time you can. Make time.

I promise this will strengthen your marriage more than anything you do. Allow the power of God to change your heart, your attitude, and your marriage. *Man Up* and take the challenge to pray for your wife, to pray with your wife, and to read the Word with her as well. This is how you start loving her as Christ loves the church.

WORKBOOK CHAPTER 2
MAN UP IN YOUR MARRIAGE

1. Read Ephesians 5:22–33. According to this, who is the spiritual head of your household? You? Your wife? Explain.

2. Do you have years of bad habits to break that are causing you to not be an Ephesians 5 husband? Name three.

3. Do you want to be the leader of your house? Why?

4. Do you listen to your wife? Truly listen? Briefly describe three conversations you have had with your wife in the last month.

5. Do you love your wife as Christ loved the church? How did He love the church?

6. Do you give yourself up for your wife? How?

7. How do you not give yourself up for her?

8. Do you pray for your wife? If not, why not?

Memory Verse—Genesis 2:24: "For this reason a man shall leave his father and his mother, and be joined to his wife; and they shall become one flesh."

This Week's Challenge 1: Give up two things that you like to do, and spend that time with your wife.

This Week's Challenge 2: Read, Pray, and Apply with your wife.

CHAPTER 3

MAN UP IN FATHERHOOD

Train up a child in the way he should go, / Even when he is old he will not depart from it. (Proverbs 22:6)

KIDS ARE LEAVING THE CHRISTIAN FAITH AT AN alarming rate. One study stated that 88 percent of the kids raised in the church are leaving the faith at or before the age of 18. This number is huge for the church. As for us fathers, it ought to show us how bad a job we are doing raising our kids in the Christian faith.

As you read in my testimony, my parents divorced when I was three. My dad was nineteen years old and still a kid. I believe that, if I'd had a kid at nineteen, I would have done the same thing. I don't blame my dad for anything bad in my life, and I love him with all my heart. But almost everything I am learning about being a father I am learning from my heavenly Father. I have many skills and traits from my dad that I pass on today to my children. But from a Christian perspective, being a father is much more than teaching skills.

If you didn't have a father or any other man in your life to show you how to be a godly man, then the Bible is the best place for you to start. God gave us His Word for us to pass on to our kids.

Deuteronomy 11:19 says, "You shall teach them to your sons, talking of them when you sit in your house and when you walk along the road and when you lie down and when you rise up." What Moses was telling us here was that we should be speaking and teaching the Word of God to our kids . . . all the time. If we want to change the direction the church is going, we begin with our kids.

In my zeal to learn God's Word in my Christian infancy, I forgot to impart what I was learning to my kids. It wasn't until later in their life that I began to read the Word to them, pray with them, and even discipline them based on the Bible. Even still, I am relying on the promise God gave us in Proverbs 22:6: "Train up a child in the way he should go, / Even when he is old he will not depart from it."

My fellow fathers, this means that you and I should be training our children in the way of the Lord. If you want your kids not to depart from the relationship with Christ when they leave the house, then train them, pray with them, and teach them what is right and wrong from the Word of God. Do not rely on the schools or even the church to be the source of their godly teaching. Make sure it comes from you.

"Fathers, do not provoke your children to anger, but bring them up in the discipline and instruction of the Lord" (Ephesians 6:4).

How To Train Your Child

"Behold, children are a gift from God" (Psalm 127:3).

Imagine if God came down from heaven and handed you a gift. Wouldn't you cherish that gift more than anything in this world? Well, he *has* handed you a gift: your children. This gift is more precious than anything that God will ever give you, outside of your salvation.

So how are you handling your gift? Are you showing your children that you believe work is more important than they are? Are you showing them that your hobbies are more important than they are? Are you showing them that your ministry is more important than they are? Your actions show your children where they rank in importance in your life.

At first, when I began to read my Bible every day, I took my reading to my office and had a private time with God. But then I realized that my kids needed to see what I was doing. So I began reading in kitchen. This way, they would see me first thing when they came down stairs to eat breakfast. Even now, when they ask what I am doing, it gives me an opportunity to tell them about the Scripture and the content of what I am reading. My goal is to someday have them both sit with me and read their Bibles as well. I am being intentional about my devotion so my kids can see their dad in the holy Word.

I want my kids to see that the only thing that will come between me and them is my quiet time with God. Not so much that I shut them out when I am reading or praying, but so that when they see me they know I am having time with my heavenly Father. My hope is that they will want the same the older they get.

We try to have a family devotion or at least a small Bible reading time with the kids before they go to bed. This is important for your children too. They need to have this quality time with you. It doesn't have to be long, but make it a point to spend some part of the evening reading the Word with your kids. Whatever the age of your children, you can find Bibles to accommodate them. Find one that works best for you and your family.

I have a friend who just reads his kids the Scripture from his Bible. He then takes the opportunity to explain what he has just read to each of them. He asks them to give examples of how they could use it in their lives. This takes a level of thought and understanding that comes only from studying the Word yourself.

The Bible tells us it is as sharp as a two-edged sword:

> For the word of God is living and active and sharper than any two-edged sword, and piercing as far as the division of soul and spirit, of both joints and marrow, and able to judge the thoughts and intentions of the heart. (Hebrews 4:12)

If you want to reach the hearts of your children, make sure you are reading the Word of God to them.

Guys, do not let this time go by. It is short and it is precious. You have the attention of your kids for only a little while. Fill their minds with as much of the Word as possible before they begin to have a mind of their own. However, it's never too late, even if you have teenagers. But you'd better be walking the walk if you want to see a change in their lives. Kids can sense hypocrisy. They will change only if they see the positive effect in your life.

Prayer Time

Maybe you are one of the many who would not be here without prayer. Some of us lived the life of a heathen, and some were brought up in the church. And some of us lived as heathens *despite* being brought up in the church. Whichever route you took to get to where you are today, you are here most likely because of prayer. You prayed, and very likely you had someone else praying for you. Your children should know without a shadow of a doubt that you are praying for them—daily.

Begin to have a time of prayer with your children. There is nothing sweeter than the prayer of a child. Christian dad, you need to encourage your child to pray. Once again, your example will be more of an influence than anything you can say. Let them see and hear you pray. Tell them the things you are praying for them. Tell them about it when a prayer is answered.

Nighttime is a great place to start. Once you have finished your family devotion, pray for your kids. Then let your kids pray. Encourage them to pray for anything they want to talk about. Don't correct them, and never laugh at their prayers—unless they mean something as a joke. God likes humor too. Let your kids open up to God in prayer. Sometimes, you may learn something you didn't know through your child's prayer, such as their fears, their pains, and their joys. It's a great opportunity to bond. Pray with your kids every night if you can. Don't let a day go by without praying for your kids.

Many years ago, I began going to my kids' rooms after they fell asleep and praying over them as they lay in their beds. I raise my hands to the heavens and thank God for them. I begin to pray for their lives, their future spouses, their fears, and for God to use them for His kingdom. This has become a humbling experience and something I look forward to every night. So . . . pray with and for your kids. This will help train them in the way they should go.

It is in your family that your discipleship begins. This is your ministry. If men in the church would take hold of the Word of God and begin to intentionally apply it to their lives, their marriages, and their children, revival would begin in America again. We could then become the godly nation that we started out to be instead of this fallen, corruptible nation that we are today.

Take this to heart: Satan is real, and he is going after your children. Just look at what is on TV, the radio, and the Internet. It appeals to the kids more than anyone. Satan is slowly infiltrating our homes through the media. We need to stand against this type of influence coming into our homes. Be careful of what your kids watch and listen to. Don't let the media become their babysitter. Guard the hearts of the little ones with the Word of God.

The teaching of dating, sex, and right and wrong should never come from the TV, movies, or music. The line of immorality is being crossed way too often with these types of entertainment, and most parents have no clue what effect it is taking on our kids. This kind of training should come from you and your wife, no one else. Don't neglect this responsibility.

Take control of teaching your children. Don't let the school system, Sunday school teacher, or even the church have control of what your kids are learning when it comes to the Bible.

Because of the teaching my wife and I have given our kids, we have had the privilege of seeing both our children come to the Cross and ask Christ to be their Lord and Savior. I also had the honor of baptizing them both. It is my responsibility to teach them everything I can about the relationship with Christ so they do not become another statistic of children leaving the faith. Men, take this responsibility seriously.

Date Night

One of my favorite times with my children is "date night." Whether it is with my daughter or my son, we set a time to go out on a date. On this date night, we go out to dinner, usually somewhere out of the ordinary. While we are at dinner, I am focused on the two of us. No phone, no game device, just us two. Talking and getting to know each other. These times are opportunities for me to see how they are doing and what they are feeling, and they are opportunities to let them know what is going on in my life.

My son is a very curious young man. Many times while we are eating he will ask, "Daddy, how's your business? Do you need any money?" He's thinking he can give me some of his allowance to help us out. I ask him, "Why do you think I need some money?" and he will reply, "I heard you and Momma talking about the business and how you said you needed sales."

By having this alone time with my son, I am able to explain to him how my business works and how he need not worry about giving Daddy his money, . That sometimes adults just talk about things so each one of us knows what's going on. Much like we are doing here in our time together.

Dates with my daughter are different. We talk about school and clothes, and we usually end up going shopping. I spend a lot of time trying to make sure I have hold of her heart for as long as I can. I show her how she should expect to be treated by her husband someday and not to expect any less than what I show her on our dates.

No matter which child I am on a date with, I want to impart to them the godly qualities and character I am learning every day. I try to show them what it looks like in action, not just in words I speak. This alone time is precious, and I am trying to get as much of it as I can.

Men, this is not rocket science. It is just time with your kids. In your busy schedule, mark off a day a month or a day a week to spend with you kids one-on-one. Start off with an hour. It will begin to turn into multiple hours. I will bet it will turn into time you can't stand to miss.

No matter how many kids you have, start making dates. When your kids see the fun-filled time they have, they will begin to make the dates for you. Enjoy them before they are gone. *Man Up!* and start becoming the godly father you were intended to be.

Workbook Chapter 3
Man Up in Fatherhood

1. List some ways that our children are being led out of our churches.
2. Are you contributing to your children leaving the church, or are you trying to stop it? In what ways?
3. How often do you talk with your kids about God, Jesus, and His Word? List ways that you can talk with them about this.
4. Are you relying on the schools or the church to teach your kids how to live?
5. What are you doing to "train up" your child or children?
6. Read Deuteronomy 6:7–9 and Matthew chapters 5–7. List several practical ways from these Scriptures that you can "train up" your child.
7. How much time have you truly spent with your children this week? What "hobbies" are in the way?
8. Do your kids see you in the Word? In prayer? How can you improve in this area?
9. Are you leading your family by example? In what ways?

This Week's Challenge 1: Turn the TV off and read and pray with your family.

This Week's Challenge 2: Read, Pray, and Apply with your wife and your children

Memory verse for this week—Ephesians 6:4: "Fathers, do not provoke your children to anger, but bring them up in the discipline and instruction of the Lord."

CHAPTER 4

MAN UP IN CHURCH

MEN ARE FALLING AWAY FROM THE CHURCH faster than any other group. In an age when it's not "cool" to go to church, men are giving more excuses than anyone. Someone once said, "Let a man-eating lion loose in a church, and he would starve to death." Look at these statistics:

» The typical U.S. congregation draws an adult crowd that's 61 percent female and 39 percent male. This gender gap shows up in all age categories.[1]

» On any given Sunday there are 13 million more adult women than men in America's churches.[2]

» This Sunday almost 25 percent of married, churchgoing women will worship without their husbands.[3]

» Midweek activities often draw 70 to 80 percent female participants.[4]

» The majority of church employees are women (except for ordained clergy, who are overwhelmingly male).[5]

» Over 70 percent of the boys who are being raised in church will abandon it during their teens and twenties. Many of these boys will never return.[6]

> » More than 90 percent of American men believe in God, and five out of six call themselves Christians. But only two out of six attend church on a given Sunday. The average man accepts the reality of Jesus Christ, but fails to see any value in going to church.[7]
> » Churches overseas report gender gaps of up to nine women for every adult man in attendance.[8]
> » Christian universities are becoming convents. The typical Christian college in the U.S. enrolls almost two women for every one man.[9]
> » Fewer than 10 percent of U.S. churches are able to establish or maintain a vibrant men's ministry.[10]

Is Church Good for Men?

Churchgoers are more likely to be married and express a higher level of satisfaction with life. Church involvement is the most important predictor of marital stability and happiness.[11]

Church involvement moves people out of poverty. It's also correlated with less depression, more self-esteem, and greater family and marital happiness.[12]

Religious participation leads men to become more engaged husbands and fathers.[13]

Teens with religious fathers are more likely to say they enjoy spending time with Dad and that they admire him.[14]

Are Men Good for the Church?

A study from Hartford Seminary found that the presence of involved men was statistically correlated with church growth, health, and harmony. Meanwhile, a lack of male participation is strongly associated with congregational decline.[15]

The numbers are astounding of how infrequently men are actually going to church, much less helping in a leadership, serving, or teaching role. But what worries me more is that many of the men who *are* in church are doing just as little as the men not going to church. Don't get me wrong: I am not preaching a works-based religion. Rather, I am looking for Spirit-filled men who are asking, "What can I do to help God's kingdom?"

There are many excuses men might give for not going to church, but the excuse I gave and the one that I hear the most is that there are hypocrites in the church. In my opinion, this is a lame excuse! If this were the true cause of why men won't go to church, then we'd also need to quit our jobs, quit our families, and quit life in general, because *there is nothing but hypocrites in this world.*

The true reason we don't want to go to church is that we are afraid to *Man Up*. We are so afraid that we are going to lose touch with the world and our sinful ways that we make up excuses about why we don't want to go to church. Satan has convinced us that going to church is for sissies. God has a different plan about church, but right now most men are not following it.

Chameleon

In the world of nature, God has created some beautiful animals. Some of these animals have great camouflage that allows them to blend into their surroundings. One of the best is the chameleon. On a bed of grass, the chameleon's skin turns green. On the earth, it turns brown. This adaptation is perfectly suited for an animal that is trying to lie low and not be seen.

In my mind, this has become the symbol of the Christian man in and out of church. At church, many Christian men try to blend into the pew, thinking that if no one sees him, he won't have to do or say anything. Outside of church, many Christian men become exactly like the world so they won't have to explain or defend why they are different. Look at what Jesus said in Revelation 3:16: "So, because you are lukewarm—neither hot nor cold—I am about to spit you out of my mouth."

God wants more from us than to just blend in. Obviously, if He says He's about to spit you out of His mouth. As a luke-warm Christian man, you are nothing more than a mouth full of snot that He will spit out. His goal for you and me is that we will be not a chameleon but light in this dark world: "Then Jesus again spoke to them, saying, 'I am the Light of the world; he who follows Me will not walk in the darkness, but will have the Light of life'" (John 8:12).

The vision you should get when you read this verse is that of a lighthouse. Back before we had GPS, sailors used lighthouses to find their way home. Even in some of the darkest storms, the lighthouse was such a bright light that those sailors were able to avoid the rocks and reach their home port.

We should be that kind of light: a spiritual light so bright that we should stand out even in the darkest hour of this world. But our light has dimmed—mostly because of our disobedience to God's Word.

How bright is your light? If you're not being intentional in your Christian walk, the darkness will overtake you. Get in the Word, pray, and become a servant in your church.

How Important Is Church?

In every generation since the death and resurrection of Christ, man has tried to devalue the church. In our current generation, man has said, "Church is a place for those who need a crutch." The world says, "Church is a place people go who can't handle things on their own." Some Christians say, "You don't have to go to a church to have church." The church as we see it today has become a joke to the world. Not because of the world, but because of Christians.

We as Christian men have let it happen. First, by our lack of action. We don't stand up for our God, we don't stand up for our faith, and we don't strive to be like the cornerstone God gave us to look up to, Jesus Christ Himself.

Second, we've let this happen by our actions. We follow the world and justify it by distorting Scripture to suit our flesh.

> For the time will come when they will not endure sound doctrine; but wanting to have their ears tickled, they will accumulate for themselves teachers in accordance to their own desires. (2 Timothy 4:3)

We continue to live in ways that are contrary to what the Bible teaches. We have become comfortable and praised by the world. How? By not doing a thing in church.

And the church is allowing it. It too has been slowly over-taken by the world. It allows the worldly influences to penetrate the church walls. Eventually, it becomes the norm, and we become numb to the effect of the world.

For example, take the movie *Forrest Gump*. It's a great movie with a happy ending. Most Christians have seen it or even own it. But if you were to take a hard look at the sexual content, nudity, taking God's name in vain, etc., it would make you blush. But the world tells us it is a sweet, fun-loving movie with a great story.

Or look at marriages. The world today says that living together is okay; you don't have to get married. But God says differently. Unfortunately, the church seems to be going along with it.

These are just two of many examples. So how important is church? It's so important that God gave his Son to die for our sins! That sounds to me like it's pretty important.

Ephesians 1:22 says: "And He put all things in subjection under His feet, and gave Him as head over all things to the church." This passage tells us that Christ is the head of the church, its source of life, its supreme ruler, and that He loves the church as a man loves his own flesh. So if that's how important it is to God, why would you and I and be so disrespectful of the church? If we are to be imitating Christ, why would we neglect the church? He died for it, but we make excuses. Not a very good imitation, is it?

The 80/20 Rule

"The Son of Man did not come to be served, but to serve, and to give His life a ransom for many" (Matthew 20:28).

As you look around your church, I would imagine that you might notice that most of the work is being done by very few people. What you see is called the Pareto Principle (also known as the 80/20 rule, the law of the vital few, and the principle of factor sparsity), which states that, for many events, roughly 80 percent of the effects come from 20 percent of the causes. In the church, you have 20 percent of the people doing 80 percent of the work. This is not a good percentage for productivity, and it causes burnout in a lot of churches.

Imagine if you worked at a 20 percent pace or if your company hired only 20 percent of its workforce to do 80 percent of its work. Neither one would last very long. Seeing this kind of statistic in the church, I can understand why six out of every 10 churches fail. After a certain amount of time, working the pace of the 20 percent club (who do most of the work), you get burned out. You just can't keep up with the demands of life, church, and family. There is nothing to do but quit.

If your church has a congregation of 100, this means that 20 people are doing the work of 80. In most churches, the remaining 20 percent of the work is just not getting done. If you have a burnout rate of 50 percent each year, that means you need 10 people each year to replace the 10 who have quit. It doesn't take a rocket scientist to figure out that you can run through church membership in a quick amount of time just by trying to fill the gaps in the church.

So let me ask this: Are you one of the 20 percent who are working all the time, or are you among the 80 percent who are watching what everyone else does?

Once again, I am not preaching a works religion. I am trying to show you that we have allowed the Christian man to forget about the personal relationship he should have with Christ. In this relationship, the Holy Spirit will deal with him about what He needs him to do for Christ's Church.

Don't think of the 80/20 rule as applying to church work; realize that it applies to *God's* work for the kingdom. If 20 percent of the church is doing 80 percent of what God has called all Christians to do—80 percent of the witnessing, 80 percent of the soul saving, and 80 percent of the disciple making—then what are the other 80 percent of the Christians doing?

Do you realize how many people we could reach for God's kingdom if the other 80 percent would stop making excuses and start sharing the gospel? We men have to step up and make a difference for God's kingdom. Stop making excuses and get in a relationship with Christ, and let Him get you involved at your church. It won't take long to get plugged in—because probably only 20 percent of the people are doing the work.

What Do I Do?

> So we, who are many, are one body in Christ, and individually members one of another. Since we have gifts that differ according to the grace given to us, each of us is to exercise them accordingly: if prophecy, according to the proportion of his faith; if service, in his serving; or he who teaches, in his teaching; or he who exhorts, in his exhortation; he who gives, with liberality; he who leads, with diligence; he who shows mercy, with cheerfulness. Let love be without hypocrisy. Abhor what is evil; cling to what is good. Be devoted to one another in brotherly love; give preference to one another in honor; not lagging behind in diligence, fervent in spirit, serving the Lord; rejoicing in hope, persevering in tribulation, devoted to prayer, contributing to the needs of the saints, practicing hospitality. (Romans 12:5–13)

Early in my Christian life, I was given a spiritual gifts survey (ask your pastor if he has one you can take), which helped me determine what gifts God had given me for His service. I believe that if I had never taken that survey, I would have been less likely to step up in the church. It gave me a guide of where to begin.

The survey tells your strengths and weakness. It is a great way to get plugged into the church. Complete a survey and take it to your pastor or teacher or accountability partner. Let the person read the survey, and then ask how you can utilize these gifts for the church. It won't take long for your gifts to magnify and glorify God when they are used for His purpose. Most of your pastors will have a spiritual gifts survey, or you can find them online.

The reason for a survey is for you to understand where God has given you strengths. Every one of us Christians has at least one gift that we can use for God's kingdom. A spiritual gift does many things for the church. First, it puts you in a place where you are less likely to get burned out. Your spiritual gift is usually stronger in things you enjoy or have naturally done most of your life. My strongest gift was exhortation, which is a speaking gift. I knew this would be high just because that was the kind of person I was. I had been in sales, and I speak in public all the time. It was just a natural fit for me.

However, God delights when He can surprise you. He can use your weakness for His glory as well. When I scored the survey, I found that my second highest gift was giving. This was a shocker to me. I am the most selfish person I know. Giving? You have got to be kidding me. But over time and many Scriptures later, I have become a giving person. With my family, my church, my money, and my work, God has slowly expanded my gifts over time.

Second, a spiritual gift gives you a point of reference for how to plug into your church. If you have a gift of exhortation, you might want to look into speaking. If it is teaching, teach a Sunday school or discipleship class. If it is administration, help in the church office. Whatever your gift is, use it!

A couple of years after I took my first spiritual gifts survey, I took another one. I wanted to see if they had changed. My first survey was shaped like a typical graph. It started out low, peaked in the middle, and dropped in the end, much like a bell curve.

My second survey, however, was much more linear. All the gifts were closer together. Over time, God was slowly molding me into the man He wanted, someone much more usable for His kingdom. To this day, He continues to show me ways I can be used through His strength and my weaknesses.

God will do the same for you. Get active in your church. Start by taking the spiritual gifts survey. Plug into the church in any way you can, where it fits with your strongest gift. Talk with your pastor to find out which direction you should take. "Therefore, my beloved brethren, be steadfast, immovable, always abounding in the work of the Lord, knowing that your toil is not in vain in the Lord" (1 Corinthians 15:58).

Pray for Your Church

Many things in life can be accomplished through prayer. As I have already stated, Christian men need to have an active prayer life. As you begin the discipline of prayer, start praying for your church. Don't pray just for growth in numbers; pray also for the spiritual growth of all your members.

Give particular attention to praying for your pastors and elders. The role of your church staff and elders is one of the most important that God has given in the church. Their account-ability for shepherding the flock needs to be covered in prayer on a daily basis. The spiritual warfare they face comes in many different forms and is consistent, so they need to be lifted up in prayer.

If the men in your church are not taking a special time before service to pray with or for the pastor, start such a move-ment yourself. Get a couple of guys together and pray with the pastor before he preaches. This type of prayer will be one of the most powerful things you can do for your pastor. It will give your pastor a comfort knowing he can deliver a sermon without the fear of being attacked by man, Satan, or himself.

"Therefore I want the men in every place to pray, lifting up holy hands, without wrath and dissension" (1 Timothy 2:8).

Just get involved in your church. It needs you as much as you need the church. Don't be a spiritual sissy. Go to church, and get involved there. *Man Up* and be a man of God in your church.

WORKBOOK CHAPTER 4
MAN UP IN THE CHURCH

1. How regular is your church attendance?
2. When you do not go, what is the reason? Do you have good reasons or are they just excuses?
3. What is the difference between a hypocrite and a sinner?
4. Do a word search through the Bible on the word lukewarm. You might use www.blueletterbible.org or www.biblegateway.com for your search.
5. What does God say about lukewarm people?
6. Are you lukewarm? In what ways?
7. How important is church to you? How does your life demonstrate how important it is to you?
8. How important does the Bible say church is?
9. Are you in the top 20 percent at your church? Or are you in the bottom 80 percent doing next to nothing?
10. What keeps you from being used in the church?
11. Read Romans 12:5–13. Respond to this passage.
12. What are your spiritual gifts?
13. Are you using your spiritual gifts in the local church?
14. Do you believe that every Christian has a spiritual gift?
15. Now that you know your gifts, how can you use them in the church and for God's kingdom?

This Week's Challenge: Pray for your church, and ask God how you can help the church further Christ's Kingdom.

Memory Verse—Matthew 20:28: "The Son of Man did not come to be served, but to serve, and to give His life a ransom for many."

CHAPTER 5

MAN UP AT WORK

"And the one on whom seed was sown among the thorns, this is the man who hears the word, and the worry of the world and the deceitfulness of wealth choke the word, and it becomes unfruitful." (Matthew 13:22)

THE STRESS OF WORK IN A MAN'S LIFE CAN become overwhelming, especially if he's focusing on nothing but work. In our generation, the world has done a good job of making sure that we focus on the *wants* in life and not the *needs,* and the American dream has become an American nightmare. With personal debt at its highest level in recorded history, it's no wonder men are taking antidepressants, drinking, and seeking anything that will numb the pain.

The Christian man is being affected more than most. His time is being pulled from every direction: work, wife, kids, hobbies, and church. The effects are starting to show in God's kingdom, because the Christian man is constantly dropping the spiritual side of life in exchange for the worldly side. This is the exact opposite of what Christ calls us to do:

Then Jesus said to His disciples, "If anyone wishes to come after Me, he must deny himself, and take up his cross and follow Me. For whoever wishes to save his life will lose it;

but whoever loses his life for My sake will find it. <u>For what</u> <u>will it profit a man if he gains the whole world and forfeits</u> <u>his soul?</u> Or what will a man give in exchange for his soul?" (Matthew 16:24–26)

The Christian man has slowly but surely, under the pressure of our consumer-driven world, exchanged his soul for the gains of the world, and he is dying a slow death. Instead of focusing on God and His kingdom, we have replaced His kingdom for our kingdom. When we focus on the material, we lose focus on the spiritual. We lose sight of God, our families, and the lost.

With this current trend, it won't take long for Christianity to be overrun by false teachings, radical religions, and complacency. We have to stop letting our work and the love of money and material things get in the way of our relationship with God.

Stopping the Snowball

In the age of technology, men have become slaves to the office. With the capability of being reached twenty-four hours a day, seven days a week, we have set ourselves up to become horrible time managers. Men are trying to constantly fit things into the schedule. Slowly, their time with God the Father is being pushed to the side.

This is causing a snowball effect. We buy more, so we need to work more. We work more, so we have less time, and we replace God's time with the world's time, and so forth and so on. Thus, the snowball keeps getting bigger.

Martin Luther once said, "If I fail to spend two hours in prayer each morning, the devil gets the victory through the day. I have so much business I cannot get on without spending three hours daily in prayer." If you feel you have so much business to do that you can't spend any time with God the Father, you are wrong. We should know better!

If you want your business to go well—and if you want more time to do the things you need to do—you must spend all the time you can with God. Don't you think that if you have Him as your partner in business, your business will go well? Don't stop at letting God be your partner—make Him your boss! And don't give in to the pressures of the world. Never let the hurriedness of your job affect your time with God. The proverbial snowball will stop once that God time is reestablished.

On-the-Job Training

As you move around your place of work this week, talking to co-workers or sitting in meetings, take a moment to look and listen to the people around you. In about two minutes, I would bet you can tell who is an intentionally living Christian and who isn't. You can tell by their body language when some kind of coarse joking is done or when someone uses foul language and they walk away or sometimes just when they speak up for the faith they believe in.

I'm not asking you to lay down judgment on what you observe in your workplace. Just because someone cusses or tells a dirty joke doesn't mean he is not a Christian. Just because someone doesn't make a scene and walk away from a dirty joke doesn't mean he's not a Christian. But what I want you to notice is how this might be a bad testimony for our faith. They have lowered the standard that God has given through His Word. So I want you to look at it and ask, "Do I look like that?"

So turn the tables now. If someone were looking at you to determine if you were an intentionally living Christian, would he see your body language when someone told a coarse joke? Would he see you walk away when someone was using foul language? Or better yet, would he see you defend your faith or witness to someone who is in need? Is your behavior at work, your on-the-job training, giving a good or bad testimony to the Christian faith?

As Christian men in the workforce today, we should be giving godly on-the-job training in everything we do. People are watching you, whether you know it or not. They look to see how you take complaints from a customer. They look to see how you deal with a rude customer or co-worker. They look to see if what you say is what you mean, so take Matthew 5:37 to heart: "Let your statement be, 'Yes, yes' or 'No, no'; anything beyond these is of evil."

When a Christian man fails to set a Christian example at work, he has lost his testimony to anyone he works with. Sound like a lot of pressure? Well, it is. No one ever said Christianity would be easy. The Christian life is not for sissies.

For us to be living intentionally as Christians, we have to behave the same at work as we do in church on Sunday morning. Don't be fake, and don't put on an air of "I have Holy Spirit joy, and you don't." You must be a real, honest, and transparent Christian who is under construction. What we want them to see in you is someone who is trying—daily—to follow the One who died for all.

When people see that we are different, that we are non-judgmental, and that we admit when we fail, they will see that we are not the stereotypical Christian the world sees. They will see the love that can only come from a spiritual source, not a pre-manufactured love that we can sometimes generate out of our own willpower. When you and I love from the flesh, it is rightly seen as fake. We must love from the Spirit. This is a complete and real love that is felt from all those we give it to.

Being a Christian in the working world is not easy, but it's a lot harder without God working actively at your side. Remember to start with God in all you do. "Whatever you do in word or deed, do all in the name of the Lord Jesus, giving thanks through Him to God the Father" (Colossians 3:17).

An Honest Living

"Wealth obtained by fraud dwindles, / But the one who gathers by labor increases it" (Proverbs 13:11).

The year 2010 brought about some major changes in the world economy. Greed has come to the forefront of business to a degree not seen in any other time in history. People are going to jail because of fraud and greed. Billions of dollars have been swindled from hard-working people. And there seems to be no end in sight. The days of the handshake business deals are all but gone now, and industry is no longer business as usual.

What happened? How have we become a nation of greed and slaves of work instead of a nation of freedom? "For the love of money is a root of all sorts of evil, and some by longing for it have wandered away from the faith and pierced themselves with many griefs" (1 Timothy 6:10).

As he was handing the Bill and Melinda Gates Foundation a check for one billion dollars, billionaire Warren Buffet said, "There is more than one way to get to heaven, but this is a great way."

The deeper we fall in love with money and the material things associated with money, the more we wander from the faith. My theory is that this is what we are seeing today. Our love for money is slowly causing us to lose sight of God almighty and the plan for salvation He has given us— Jesus Christ, the one and only way to heaven (hopefully someone will tell this to Mr. Buffet). No amount of work or money is going to get us close to heaven. We can't buy our way in and we can't be "good" enough!

But what is happening is that we have become so in love with money that we have lost sight of what is important, and in some cases we have become dishonest when it comes to making more money. When you and I love something more than we love God, it becomes an idol. Remember the first Commandment? Thou shalt have no other gods before me. Is money your god? Is work your god?

My friend, you have to strike a balance in this part of your life. An imbalance here will cause you to lose balance everywhere else. Make sure you are honest and that you do an honest day's work, of course, but do not let the love of money become your god.

Each man will have a different way of balancing his life, and I wish I could give you a formula to help you with this. But the best way I have found is to get God involved in your work, first and foremost. In daily Bible study and prayer, let Him know what you need. Once this becomes a part of your life, balance will begin to happen. Be strong in your Christian faith. Follow God in your work. And be honest.

Man Up and Rest

"Remember the Sabbath day, to keep it holy" (Exodus 20:8).

In the rat race we're in today, very few men are taking the time to actually rest. I am not talking about sleeping; I am talking about a complete day of rest. A day when the most you do is go to church, go home to eat, and just rest—without the

TV or other distractions. Before you say, "It can't be done!" let me ask you this: Have you ever tried it?

Up until 1980, the U.S. had a law that would not allow businesses to be open on Sunday. It was called the Blue Law. I am just old enough to remember a time when nothing was open on Sunday so you had to be prepared for it. You had to be sure gas was in the car and milk was in the fridge. Families got together to have a Sunday lunch. It was peaceful and a time to enjoy a day of rest.

Then we became so greedy that we had to make money on Sunday. Since then, life has actually become harder for most, our country is swimming in debt, and moral decay is becoming worse every day. Since 1980, life has become a hectic and almost unbearable rat race. To the point that the number one prescribed medicine is antidepressants. A study done by the government states the following:

> According to a government study, antidepressants have become the most commonly prescribed drugs in the United States. They're prescribed more than drugs to treat high blood pressure, high cholesterol, asthma, or headaches. CNN's Elizabeth Cohen discusses the CDC study on antidepressants.
>
> In its study, the U.S. Centers for Disease Control and Prevention looked at 2.4 billion drugs prescribed in visits to doctors and hospitals in 2005. Of those, 118 million were for antidepressants.
>
> High blood pressure drugs were the next most-common with 113 million prescriptions.
>
> The use of antidepressants and other psychotropic drugs—those that affect brain chemistry—has skyrocketed

over the last decade.

Adult use of antidepressants almost tripled between the periods 1988–1994 and 1999–2000.

Between 1995 and 2002, the most recent year for which statistics are available, the use of these drugs rose 48 percent, the CDC reported.[1]

Do you think this is a coincidence? I don't. Society has taken out a day of rest just so we can get even more stuff we don't need. The more stuff we think we need, the more we buy; the more we buy, the more we owe; the more we owe, the more we work. Even to the point that we work on Sundays, the Lord's day.

God commanded us to rest. It is His fourth Commandment. Yet for some time now we have disobeyed this law. Even churches are guilty of this. God rested—why don't we?

Let me give you some reasons why you need to rest.

Of the entire list of Ten Commandments that God gave to Moses, the only thing He told us to remember was the Sabbath (Exodus 20:8). Why should we remember it? Maybe because God, in His infinite wisdom, knew that someday we would forget it. He knew we would succumb to the worldly ways and forget to rest.

Jesus reminded us again that this day, the Sabbath day, was for mankind: "Jesus said to them, 'The Sabbath was made for man, and not man for the Sabbath'" (Mark 2:27). It's a time when we need to rest, to take a moment from our busy schedules and look upon the Lord for just a moment.

So why is it so hard? Well, we are hardheaded, for one thing. We believe we can dictate how we live, how we work, and how we rest. I used to say, "I'll rest when I am dead."

With an attitude like that, it won't take long to get that kind of rest.

Here are three reasons you should remember the Sabbath.

The Body Needs It

The older I get, the more I understand that my body just can't do what it used to. Every day our bodies are growing old, some faster than others. As we continue to work, continue to play, and continue to get caught up in what the world calls life, our days are getting shorter, and our bodies are more tired.

Below is a graph I made of the average day for the average Christian man in America in the early part of the twenty-first century. As you will notice, this is very basic. There are no sports to take the kids to, no before- or after-work meetings, no church meetings, no doctor visits, etc. My point is to get you to understand that you are not Superman. You need to learn to take a day of rest, a holy day for you and your family.

Average Day

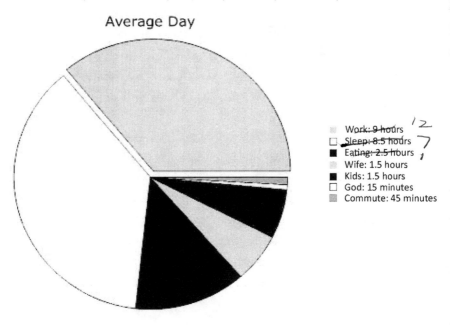

Work: 9 hours   12
Sleep: 8.5 hours   7
Eating: 2.5 hours   1
Wife: 1.5 hours
Kids: 1.5 hours
God: 15 minutes
Commute: 45 minutes

Perhaps you don't fit on this chart. Maybe you work more than forty hours a week and have a commute that is longer than twenty-five minutes. Maybe you sleep more like six hours per day. And the more kids you have, the more events you have to attend. And so forth and so on. But it's still a good graph for our discussion.

As you may notice, this graph makes no room for extracurricular activities—no fun. You may ask, "Where can I get more time?" You can't, but you can learn to use your time wisely. You can learn to take time for a day of rest.

My friend, your body needs to rest. Test this out, and see if God won't give you supernatural strength and supernatural time to do the things you need to do. Give Him this one day when you don't do anything but worship Him . . . and rest.

The Mind Needs It

Scientific studies have been done on how much a person can work before the effort starts to become a detriment to the person and the job. Study after study states that a person who does not take time off will actually become less intelligent, and his moral standards will drop. God knew this the moment He made creation, so He gave us the example for us to follow:

> By the seventh day God completed His work which He had done, and He rested on the seventh day from all His work which He had done. Then God blessed the seventh day and sanctified it, because in it He rested from all His work which God had created and made. (Genesis 2:2–3)

God knew before people ever did that they would need a day of rest. He knew, all the way back in the beginning of time, that man is just dumb enough to think he doesn't need it and that he can mentally handle the things the world would throw at him.

Science supports God's idea of a day of rest. By analyzing workers' blood, scientists have seen that, during the workers' efforts through the week, they recovered in one night's rest only five-sixths of the ounce of oxygen they consumed in that day's labor. Each morning found the workers one-sixth of an ounce short. And this accumulated every day, so that by the end of the week, the workers' vitality was run down.

The Lord's Day is a physiological necessity for the restoration of that one ounce. When a man presumes to be smarter than God, he usually pays the penalty in these ways: nervous breakdowns, insomnia, stress, and/or nervous debility.

My fellow Christian man, your mind needs the rest, as well. Learn to turn it off. I have begun this process of a Sabbath, and I can tell you, it's not easy. The first Sunday I took for myself and my family, I was freaking out. I felt guilty for taking a day for myself, and I felt as if I were forgetting something. I opened the Word of God and read aloud to make my mind focus on Him. By the end of the day, I was looking forward to the next Sunday.

The Soul Needs It

Many Sunday mornings I awaken, and I'm already mad at the world. I don't have any desire whatsoever to go to church. I angrily get ready and head out the door to go to church. After an argument with the wife and a spat with the kids, I arrive at church . . . ready to worship God. As I walk into the church, I try to walk straight to my seat so no one will talk to me. But it never fails that someone will catch me and give me a hug or a kind word. And then it just refreshes my soul.

This is the true nature of church. This is how church should be every Sunday. Not that we come all mad, but it's a place to be encouraged and a place that gives rest to your soul.

Having rest for your body and rest for your mind will do you no good if you don't also take time to get rest for your soul. Once again, the best example is that of Jesus Christ: "And He came down to Capernaum, a city of Galilee, and He was teaching them on the Sabbath" (Luke 4:31). Even Jesus took time to go to church on the Sabbath.

Don't make your day of rest just about you. Make it more about the One who led you from slavery, the One who set you free. Spend time in fellowship with other believers and soaking in the day of worship along with a day of rest.

I challenge you to just try it: for your body, mind, and soul. *Man Up* and learn to balance your life.

WORKBOOK CHAPTER 5
MAN UP AT WORK

1. What is the difference between wants and needs in reference to your stuff?

2. What did Jesus say about "losing life" and "gaining life" in Matthew 16?

3. Do you really believe what Jesus said? Is there no room for me to fulfill my "little wants"? Explain your answer.

4. What have you lost focus of (family, church, life . . .)?

5. Where is your focus?

6. Have you ever just sat down and tried to evaluate what should be your focus? Do so now.

7. Joseph Allenine, an English pastor, arose at four and began his business of praying until eight. If he heard other workers going about their business before he was up, he would exclaim, "Oh, how this shames me! Does my Master not deserve more than theirs?" Who is your master? You are a slave to something; what are you a slave to?

8. Are you giving godly on-the-job training to anyone? Who, and in what ways?

9. Describe how you act at work. Would anyone notice if you were a Christian?

10. Are you doing Colossians 3:17? In what ways?

11. Explain what rest means to you. What does rest mean biblically?

12. What are you doing instead of resting?

13. What is taking the place of worship to your Master?

This Week's Challenge: Turn off your phone and computer for two hours each day to be with your family. Take the Lord's Day and do nothing but go to church and spend time with the family. (Do not go out to eat; eat at home.)

Memory Verse—Matthew 16:24–26: "Then Jesus said to His disciples, 'If anyone wishes to come after Me, he must deny himself, and take up his cross and follow Me. For whoever wishes to save his life will lose it; but whoever loses his life for My sake will find it. For what will it profit a man if he gains the whole world and forfeits his soul? Or what will a man give in exchange for his soul?'"

CHAPTER 6

MAN UP AND BE ACCOUNTABLE

> My brethren, if any among you strays from the truth and one turns him back, let him know that he who turns a sinner from the error of his way will save his soul from death and will cover a multitude of sins. (James 5:19–20)

PASTORS, POLITICIANS, AND CELEBRITIES ARE ALL falling like dominos. Scandals, affairs, drug abuse, and more are taking them out one by one. It's true from Jim Bakker to Ted Haggard, from Bill Clinton to Elliot Spitzer, and, well, take your pick as far as celebrities go. Men are falling from grace faster than they rose, and this is happening closer to home more often than we like to see.

Leaders in your own church are falling victim to the devil's deceit. Every so often we see men in positions of authority in our church fall to the temptation of the flesh, and it is killing the witness we are supposed to have to the world. All because of one thing: the lack of *accountability*.

ac·count·a·bil·i·ty—noun 1. the state of being accountable, liable, or answerable (www.dictionary.com, accessed 11/1/2011).

In our culture men are falling away from the faith faster than at any other time in history. The world tells us, "You can do it on your own," and it gets us to believe the statement so much that we *try* it on our own—only to fail, in many cases. There is nothing wrong with trying to succeed or accomplish great things, but what is wrong is thinking we don't need anyone to help or to look after us in the process.

Having no accountability in your Christian walk will lead to a spiritual demise—guaranteed.

Men have brought the "I can do it on my own" attitude into the church, and it is slowly killing the church and the people in it. We have taken accountability out of the process of discipleship, and it is eroding the responsibility of the Christian man. Now we no longer feel that each of us should be someone who is different, someone set apart from the world.

You and I need to be accountable in our personal walk with Jesus, accountable to our families, accountable to our church, and accountable to each other. But this step is hard and will require determination.

It is my opinion that if the guys I mentioned earlier had had some sort of accountability program set up for them, they would have been less likely to fall from grace. It is also my opinion that, even if they'd started with an accountability program in place, you could look back on their lives and see a slow fade from when they were accountable to someone to when that accountability became nonexistent.

We must embrace an accountability program in the church and in our lives. We must establish around us godly relationships in which we can be honest and open, relationships in which we can challenge one another in our daily walk. Men have all the same problems as other men, so why do we act like no one else knows what we are going through?

Embrace this. Stop being a spiritual sissy and learn to share your struggles with another godly man. Learn to hold someone accountable and learn to be accountable.

Accountability for Sissies 101

"When the apostles returned, they gave an account to [Jesus] of all that they had done. Taking them with Him, He withdrew by Himself to a city called Bethsaida" (Luke 9:10).

As always, we can learn the most about how we should be by looking at Christ's example. For three years, Jesus took twelve ordinary men like you and me and discipled them in such a way that they were later able to go out and change the world.

What He did more than anything else was keep them accountable to His teaching and to their actions. Many times in Scripture Jesus had to rebuke, correct, and discipline the disciples. Some more than others. He was continually holding them accountable. Notice that Jesus preached to the masses, but He taught and discipled only twelve. This is the ultimate form of accountability.

Imagine spending three years with the same guys. There is no way the apostles could've gotten away with anything in a scenario like that. Not to mention that Jesus knew their hearts. But if you look around your church, you can see guys with whom you have been going to church for more years than Jesus spent with the apostles. These are guys you spend hours a week with, and yet you have no clue who they are. Why? Because, as I said earlier, we think we can do it on our own.

Jesus knew, when He sent the apostles out to witness, that they couldn't do it on their own. They needed an accountability partner. So He instituted a New Testament buddy system: "And He summoned the twelve and began to send them out in pairs, and gave them authority over the unclean spirits" (Mark 6:7).

Jesus knew that sending out individuals with this kind of power would lead only to disaster. Apostles proclaiming the gospel in their own name would have given us a different Bible. But Jesus didn't send them on their own; He sent them in teams. He took away the probability of them failing—by giving them accountability.

You and I should use the model Christ gave us. We are not strong enough to keep from failing. We need each other to keep us in check.

At its core, accountability is the honest and open dialogue of one Christian brother to another. You and I should *never* have an accountability partner who is a woman. I'm not saying you can't talk with your wife. But if you are not married, or even if you are unhappily married, never have a woman for an accountability partner.

Accountability is intimate, and people can become vulnerable. A situation could arise that would put you in a precarious position. To state it bluntly, there are some things you should never discuss with a woman, including your wife. I am not saying you need to keep secrets, but there are struggles men go through that (at the beginning, at least) your wife doesn't need to know about. Example: impure thoughts. Men can relate; most women cannot. You start telling your wife you are having impure thoughts, and she is going to start getting jealous and worrying about something that will probably lead to nothing.

On the other hand, you tell another man you are having these thoughts, and he can lead you to Scriptures, testimony about his own life, and ways he got over it. Or maybe you both are dealing with it and can both search for help, even to the point that you get pastoral help together. Once you have begun the process of solving or identifying the source of your impure thoughts, or any other sin for that matter, then you can think about telling your wife, especially the part about how you have overcome it. She will be more likely to accept the information knowing you have overcome it and have a plan to deal with it.

After having problems with pornography and impure thoughts for most of my life, I discussed this with my accountability partner. He advised me to go through certain steps in order to tame my mind and my addiction to pornography. These thoughts and actions were so ingrained that it took time for me to deal with them.

But after that time, I talked with my wife about it. I let her know about the problem I was having and how, through accountably, Scripture, and prayer, I had begun to deal with it. To my surprise, her response was, "What can I do to help?" This opened a dialogue with her that led to many more conversations of difficulties for both of us. We worked on them together.

My hope is that, in the near future, you too will be able to talk things over with your wife. But start with another man, maybe someone who has been through the same issues. Begin the process of working them out, and only then talk with your wife about them.

As you become open to the idea of accountability with someone you trust you will begin to talk about the struggles in your life and in your accountability partner's life. These struggles are sometimes impure thoughts, issues at home, or issues at work. Sometimes they're even blatant sins that you or your partner is continuing to live in. The point of doing this is to get to know the person well enough that you can sense without being told when this person is having problems.

All men have only five problems: sex, women, work, kids, and money. That's how simplistic we are. So somewhere out there, there is an accountability partner for you. You just have to want it. We will continue to have these problems until we lay them at the feet of Jesus. Get someone to help you. Begin the process together.

I began this process several years ago with a good friend of mine. He was about ten years younger than I was, but for some reason we really connected. He had been raised in the church, and I had just been born again. We began meeting weekly. At those first few meetings, we just talked, getting to know each other. After that, we moved on into Scripture.

The deeper we moved into Scripture, the deeper our talks became. I remember one particular time we met. I was struggling with an issue. We started as usual with the niceties. Read our Scripture. Then he asked me, "How's it going?"

"Great," I said. "And you?"

He looked at me carefully. "Liar."

"What do you mean?" I asked.

"I can see it written all over you. Something's wrong."

Of course, he was right. I then opened up and began to get the world off my shoulders. Come to find out, he had the same problem.

Later that summer, we taught a men's class in which we shared our struggles. Through that, we had twelve to fifteen guys open up about their struggles as well. It was great. All because of accountability.

When you get to know someone that closely, you will learn to know each other and begin to sense when something's wrong.

Finding the Right Person

Accountability is not easy. Neither is finding the right person to be accountable with. Perhaps you have that friend whom you know you can talk to. Or maybe you can't yet think of anyone you can trust. When looking for that person, start with prayer—deep heartfelt prayer. Ask God to place in your path that one man who can help you or whom you can help. Someone whom you can trust with the most intimate things on your heart, your deepest secrets. Ask God to help you open up to whoever that person may be and vice versa.

When Jesus began to choose His disciples, look at what Scripture says He did:

> It was at this time that He went off to the mountain to pray, and He spent the whole night in prayer to God. And when day came, He called His disciples to Him and chose twelve of them, whom He also named as apostles. (Luke 6:12–13)

Jesus spent the whole night *praying.* Don't you think He could have just gone out without praying and chosen twelve guys, and they would have been the right ones? Yeah, but I believe that night of prayer wasn't for Him; it was for us. It was an example to show us that, no matter the situation, no matter how sure we are, we need to pray first.

Finding an accountability partner needs the same kind of prayer. This is someone you are going to hand your heart to. You need to make sure it's the right person.

But maybe you're saying, "I'm not that kind of guy—I don't open up to anyone." I say, "Get over yourself!" Accountability is a process of discipleship, and we are all called to disciple. So, if you are going to follow Jesus' last command as He left this earth, you are going to have to get over yourself. So start praying for God to help you in this area.

"He who neglects discipline despises himself, / But he who listens to reproof acquires understanding" (Proverbs 15:32).

I do want to warn you, though: there are wolves in sheep's clothing. The example I gave about my first accountability partner is an ideal situation. I also had an accountability partner who, I found out later, was a gossip and liar.

Proverbs 20:19 says, "He who goes about as a slanderer reveals secrets, Therefore do not associate with a gossip."

Be prepared to be hurt, but do not let it stop you from being accountable to someone. We all get hurt in our jobs, our marriages, and our lives, but it doesn't stop us from keeping on. So don't let this either. Once you find the right person, you and your accountability partner's lives will be changed.

Now What?

"Therefore, confess your sins to one another, and pray for one another so that you may be healed. The effective prayer of a righteous man can accomplish much" (James 5:16).

After prayerful consideration, you have found your partner. Now it's time to begin the journey of accountability.

The idea behind accountability is to have someone you can confide in. Start by setting ground rules, such as a time and a place to meet, agreeing that what is said here stays here, being courteous of each other's time, and not being judgmental. Agree to use Scripture or testimonies—not opinions—to help with problems. Agree to not gossip and to be truthful and that each person should contribute to the time of accountability. In some cases you may want to use an accountability agreement form (you can find one in the back of the book). There are many other guidelines, but these are just a few to help you get going in the process.

After getting to know each other, share your testimonies. You can even use the testimony that you wrote in the first chapter of *Man Up!* It's good to know the background of the other person when it comes to your stories of salvation. Be detailed in your stories and share the good and the bad about your Christian walk. No one has a picture-perfect walk. If he claims to have one, you may want to find another partner, because he's not going to be honest anyway.

Then open the Scriptures. Find topics that one or both of you are struggling with, and read everything the Word says about it.

For example, if the topic is immorality, start in Proverbs 5. Take time to understand what the Word is saying. Learn how it applies to either of your situations. And then apply it to your lives in order for you to overcome the temptations of life. The Word will convict like the two-edged sword it is (Hebrews 4:12). No matter what anyone says, either you or your partner or the greatest preacher alive, nothing will convict you like the Word of God will. You have to be in the Word of God every time you meet with you accountability partner. It will be a wasted meeting if you're not.

And don't stop meeting. Romans 12:10 says, "Be devoted to one another in brotherly love; give preference to one another in honor." As you both learn to grow with each other, you need to begin to disciple others.

Man Up, and learn to open up!

WORKBOOK CHAPTER 6
MAN UP AND BE ACCOUNTABLE

1. Define accountability in your own words.
2. Do you have anyone in your life to whom you are accountable? If not, why not? There could only be two reasons why you do not have anyone in your life: 1) you didn't know you should have someone in your life to hold you accountable, or 2) you don't want anyone knowing your secrets. What's your response to that?
3. How did Jesus send out the disciples? Why would He have done it this way? How can we use this model today?
4. List some reasons why you want an accountability partner.
5. List some reasons why you do not want an accountability partner?
6. Have you asked God to show you a partner to be accountable to? If not, do so now.
7. List the steps you need to take once you find your accountability partner.
8. What do you think are the most important steps for accountability?
9. What do you think accountability leads to?

This Week's Challenge: Ask God to show you an accountability partner.

Memory Verse—James 5:16: "Therefore, confess your sins to one another, and pray for one another so that you may be healed. The effective prayer of a righteous man can accomplish much."

CHAPTER 7

MAN UP AND DISCIPLE

"Go therefore and make disciples of all the nations, baptizing them in the name of the Father and the Son and the Holy Spirit." (Matthew 28:19)

AS I READ THE NEW TESTAMENT, THE DEFINITION I get of a disciple is this: a person who is a born-again believer, who is obedient, who bears fruit, who glorifies God, who has joy, who loves others, who denies himself, and who is committed to fulfilling the Great Commission. The problem with this definition is that people like this are almost nonexistent in the modern-day church.

The great evangelistic movement of the twentieth century has done more harm than good to discipleship. Discipleship has been given a back seat to evangelism. The mind set of "Get 'em saved and move 'em out" is killing the church today. It has left us with a plethora of "back row" (non-growing) Christians who are just taking up space.

Concerning him we have much to say, and it is hard to explain, since you have become dull of hearing. For though by this time you ought to be teachers, you have need again for someone to teach you the elementary principles of the oracles of God, and you have come to need milk and not solid food. For everyone who partakes only of milk is not accustomed to the word of righteousness, for he is an infant. But solid food is for the mature, who because of practice have their senses trained to discern good and evil. (Hebrews 5:11–14)

Jesus' explanation of the parable of the sower is the perfect example of the evangelism movement today. Many are preaching the Word, and many are hearing it, but very few are teaching others how to use it. Discipleship should be a process in which we teach the Word to someone who has heard it but who doesn't know how to apply it.

"The one on whom seed was sown on the rocky places, this is the man who hears the word and immediately receives it with joy; yet he has no firm root in himself, but is only temporary, and when affliction or persecution arises because of the word, immediately he falls away" (Matthew 13:20–21).

Only through application can you learn to hold onto the Word when persecution and affliction start. New converts and complacent Christians need this in their lives so that they will not fall away when trials come. If we stop at evangelism, we risk the chance of root growth on top of the soil instead of a thriving plant with deep roots.

What Is Discipleship?

Discipleship in its purist form is the teaching of what you *are*. This process shows a new believer how to do discipleship, not just hear discipleship. This should start the moment your personal relationship with Christ has begun, which I talked about all the way back in the first chapter.

Once your personal relationship is in full force, your discipleship ministry should start with your family. As this process continues, you would then begin the search for an accountability partner. As you begin this relationship, the two of you should evolve the process of accountability to include others such as new converts or back-row Christians. These new converts are not to be involved in your personal accountability, but can be discipled as an offshoot of the growth you are getting from your personal relationship with God and having someone keep you accountable in your personal walk.

Side note: Do not get accountability confused with discipleship. Accountability is for your personal walk as a man. Discipleship is for you to teach your walk to a man who has no clue what the Christian walk looks like.

Your disciple should know about you what Paul says about himself:

> Not that I have already obtained it or have already become perfect, but I press on so that I may lay hold of that for which also I was laid hold of by Christ Jesus. Brethren, I do not regard myself as having laid hold of it yet; but one thing I do: forgetting what lies behind and reaching forward to what lies ahead, I press on toward the goal for the prize of the upward call of God in Christ Jesus. (Philippians 3:12–14)

As the one who is doing the discipling, you are not perfect, although your goal should be perfection.

Do not feel you have to have it all together to start discipling. You must know and use the Word in your life before you start discipling someone else, but you don't have to be a Bible scholar.

Process of Discipleship

"Therefore be imitators of God, as beloved children" (Ephesians 5:1).

There are two words that we should look at when talking about discipleship: *imitate* and *example*. Jesus and Paul used these words more than anyone else in the New Testament. Jesus and Paul both should be imitated and used as our examples of the purist form of discipleship: Jesus as disciple of God and Paul as disciple of Jesus.

When we begin the process of our discipleship our gauge, our goal, and our measuring stick should be these two. One example should be Jesus in the way He led a perfect life, in the way He did not get distracted from His purpose, and in the way that He showed love for all.

We should imitate Paul in his great example as a sinful man who, at his very core, fought and struggled with the flesh, but overcame because he followed the One who came before him, Jesus Christ. We as sinful men will struggle just like Paul did and will fail more often than Paul did, because we have not truly sold out to God as Paul had. The more we sell out to Jesus the way Paul did, the more our walk will look like his.

When following Christ, our ultimate mentor, we should imitate everything from His life as well as the example He left His apostles. Through His example, we see the kind of life a Christian should live:

> For you have been called for this purpose, since Christ also suffered for you, leaving you an example for you to follow in His steps, who committed no sin, nor was any deceit found in his mouth; and while being reviled, He did not revile in return; while suffering, He uttered no threats, but

kept entrusting Himself to Him who judges righteously; and He Himself bore our sins in His body on the cross, so that we might die to sin and live to righteousness; for by His wounds you were healed. For you were continually straying like sheep, but now you have returned to the Shepherd and Guardian of your souls. (1 Peter 2:21–25)

I call discipleship a process. When we are transformed to the new creature from our old self, we are in no condition to be disciplining anyone until we learn how to apply the Word to our lives. Paul was discipled by Ananias and Barnabas before he began to spread the gospel. We all need a Barnabas in our lives. Then, once we become a Paul—a mature disciple—through the teachings of our Barnabas, we need to find our Timothy: someone we can begin discipling. That is the process. In simple terms, it's addition: one plus one plus one plus one.

Hopefully, you will disciple the next Timothy, who will preach to a church, or the next Paul, who will live his life traveling the world proclaiming the Good News. Or better yet, you will disciple a man who is struggling in his life, and then what he learns from this process will make him a better man, a better husband, and a better father. That is the process of discipleship.

The knowledge of the Word, the application as you live it, and the testimony of the process should be like a river flowing from you to others. It should never be a pool or a reservoir in which you store it.

The power a dam gives off doesn't come from millions of gallons of water it is holding back. The power of a dam comes at the moment it opens the floodgates and lets the water out. That's the real power. Open your floodgates of the Word: the application of the Bible and the power of prayer. Stop being a sissy. *Man Up* and find a Barnabas to teach you, then find your Paul or Timothy to teach.

Seed, Tree, Fruit

Discipleship can be as simple as someone watching your walk or as in-depth as a three-year Bible study done one-on-one. But in order to truly understand our role in the process of discipleship, I want us to look at the seed, the tree, and the fruit it produces.

For a tree to grow a seed must first be planted. Every Christian has had the proverbial seed planted when it comes to our salvation. Someone at some time showed us kindness, gave us a good word, or prayed with or for us. Maybe without us even knowing it, the Word of God entered into our soul or mind, and it planted a thought from God. Over time the seed began to spout and started to root. The time between the seed being planted and the spouting can be years, but it eventually spouts. Mustard seeds sprout within one day, and some trees take over a year to sprout.

In 1996, my uncle Mark, a good Christian man, father, and husband, wrote me a note. He and I were only ten years apart, and we hung out quite a bit. He knew I was an atheist, and he didn't try to push too hard when it came to Christianity. But something spurred him to write me a note. In that note was a simple and humble message. The message basically said that he didn't want to come off as a Bible beater, but he wanted me to know that the God who had saved him and loved him would save and love me if I would just let Him in. He died a few years later without ever seeing me come to Christ. But he planted a seed.

In 1999, a good friend of mine named John Allen did the same. (See the letter in the back of the book.) He told me that, as he was coming back from a Promise Keepers event, he felt moved to send me a Bible and to let me know he loved me. I read the letter and put the Bible (still in its box) on the shelf— until my salvation in 2003. I never read the Bible, but he'd still planted a seed.

As disciples, we should be planting seeds. How many seeds are you planting? This seed-planting part of discipleship is called evangelism. And we all need to be doing it. Plant the seed, and let God start to grow it.

But this book is about the tree and the fruit, not the seed. This book is for the Christian man who has already had that seed planted. Now he is a tree that is bearing little or no fruit. This book is to get men motivated to move and stop being spiritual sissies in sharing the Good News. We should be excited that we have the opportunity to share something that will save lives, heal marriages, expand the church, and raise godly children. It's the message of Christ.

But a tree with branches that are not producing fruit will eventually be taken away, and that's what has happened to the men in our churches today. They are not bearing fruit, and God will eventually take them away.

"I am the true vine, and My Father is the vinedresser. Every branch in Me that does not bear fruit, He takes away; and every branch that bears fruit, He prunes it so that it may bear more fruit. You are already clean because of the word which I have spoken to you. Abide in Me, and I in you. As the branch cannot bear fruit of itself unless it abides in the vine, so neither can you unless you abide in Me. I am the vine, you are the branches; he who abides in Me and I in him, he bears much fruit, or apart from Me you can do nothing." (John 15:1–5)

I don't know how He will "take them away," but we may already be seeing it by the way our men are leaving the church. God may be letting the world—or even the enemy—have them, but we need to change this and change it fast. We need to become men who are pruned.

Men are pruned when they are bearing fruit. As we begin to spread God's message to others, we begin to bear fruit. And as we continue to grow in God's Word, the Word itself begins to prune us. It's the process of *sanctification*. That process should be that you are in more of a right standing with God today than you were yesterday. This is how we are pruned.

Then, as we become more faithful and fruitful, we learn to honor God, and our Lord is glorified more. God loves to see men in right standing with Him, righteous men willing to share all they know and all they are with others. That is discipleship.

It is time for us to stand together and learn to be great disciples to all those who know us. It is time for us to be great men of faith and for us to take a stand and stop being spiritual sissies. *Man Up* and spread God's Word.

How To Do Discipleship

Now it's time to find someone to disciple. What do you do first? Once again, you pray. You pray that God will place someone in your path, in your mind, or on your heart whom you can help learn more about what God wants for him.

This process is not much different from that of being an accountability partner, except that now you are the teacher. You are taking the things you are learning in your personal walk with Christ, the knowledge of God's Word from your daily devotions, and the whispers from God's Spirit that you've heard in your prayer times, and you are imparting them to another man who needs to hear it from an intentionally living Christian man.

Research the many books that offer help with discipleship. Choose topics, people, or areas of interest, and take your disciple on a journey that will change his life.

And don't stop. When the man you are discipling is ready to start discipling someone himself, move on to the next back-row Christian. God bless you. My prayer is that you become a great disciple maker.

Workbook Chapter 7
Man Up and Disciple

1. What does the term disciple mean to you?
2. What does Jesus mean in Matthew 28:19 when He says "Go make disciples"?
3. Have you been discipled? Explain how it worked.
4. Who are you imitating? Who should you imitate? What brought you to this point of deciding whom to imitate?
5. List several people from the Bible who you think would be good for you to imitate.
6. Read Jesus' Sermon on the Mount (Matthew 5–7) and give several examples how you can imitate Christ.
7. The Christian life, like discipleship, is a process called sanctification. How have you been sanctified? How are you being sanctified now?
8. If you have been discipled, you're ready to disciple someone else. Who might you tap on the shoulder to disciple? How would you do that? What keeps you from discipling someone?

This Week's Challenge: Find someone to disciple you, or find someone to disciple.

Memory Verse—Proverbs 27:17: "Iron sharpens iron, So one man sharpens another."

CHAPTER 8

PUT UP OR SHUT UP

ITS TIME MEN PUT UP OR SHUT UP. I HOPE THIS book stirs you to the point of being challenged. I have thrown down the gauntlet. I have called you a spiritual sissy.

This is the charge I leave you with. What are you going to do with the challenge? Are you going to *Man Up*? Will you put up a fight and stand up for what should matter most in your life and in the lives around you? Or are you going to keep living as a spiritual sissy?

If it is the latter, then shut up. Jesus challenged you like this:

> "Go therefore and make disciples of all the nations, baptizing them in the name of the Father and the Son and the Holy Spirit, teaching them to observe all that I commanded you; and lo, I am with you always, even to the end of the age." (Matthew 28:19–20)

Sounds like a challenge to me. And I bet most of us have failed at it. We Christian men should be honoring God by living the Word He has given us, but we have failed. We have failed to fight for our faith, stand up for our families, be an example in our church and workplaces, and make disciples. The time is now to make a change.

I challenge you! I implore you! Seek the Word, pray, and apply it daily to your life. That is the only way we will change the world.

Do you believe Genesis 1:26: "Then God said, 'Let Us make man in Our image, according to Our likeness'"—do you believe that? If so, then you have to see that God did not create us to be spiritual sissies. We are to be *men!* In His image! Godly, spiritual men who are willing to lay down our lives for our personal relationship with Christ, our marriages, our kids, our church, our work, and the betterment of our fellow man. God is not a sissy nor should any man He made in His image be a sissy. Now is the time to put up or shut up.

Leave behind the life of a spiritual sissy. Step into the role of a Christ-centered, God-fearing man, and let's change the world. It's not too late for you to repent, for the church to repent, or even for this nation to repent. Jesus said, "The time is fulfilled, and the kingdom of God is at hand; repent and believe in the gospel" (Mark 1:15). We should do all we can for the kingdom in the time we have.

God bless you as you stop being a spiritual sissy! Remember, *read, pray,* and *apply.* Now is the time . . . *Man Up!*

WORKBOOK CHAPTER 8
PUT UP OR SHUT UP

1. Who are you going to do it with? List some men who you can do the following with:

   Accountability:

   Discipleship:

2. List the Spiritual Sissies you know to give a copy of this book to:

This Week's Challenge: Get a plan together of what, how, and with whom you are going to battle. This walk is a battle; if you are not prepared you will fail. Soldiers go to battle with soldiers. God has giving you a battle plan in His Word, read it. Pray that God will bless your plans and the soldiers you are going into battle with. Put your plan into practice. Apply your battle plan.

Memory Verse—Matthew 28:18–20: "And Jesus came up and spoke to them, saying, 'All authority has been given to Me in heaven and on earth. Go therefore and make disciples of all the nations, baptizing them in the name of the Father and the Son and the Holy Spirit, teaching them to observe all that I commanded you; and lo, I am with you always, even to the end of the age.'"

THE 30 DAY
MAN UP CHALLENGE
AND DEVOTION

The 30-day Man Up! Challenge: Are you man enough to step up to the challenge? Remember: Pray, read, and apply. During this challenge you will need to pray and study the Word of God, pray to stay in fellowship with God, and then apply to your life the truths you have learned from God. The best evangelism is living an obedient Christ-centered life. Time to *Man Up!*

Days 1–6—PERSONAL
Challenge: Pray about and write out your testimony (if you didn't already do so in the first chapter.

Day 1
- » Pray about and write out your testimony.
- » Begin reading your Bible and continue doing so through the entire thirty days. Read Acts 1 and Proverbs 1 (don't just read it; follow the how-to study guide).
- » Pray and ask God to forgive you of your sins and your spiritual sissiness.
- » Begin your prayer journal.

Day 2

» Continue to pray about your testimony and edit your original.
» Read Acts 2 and Proverbs 2.
» Write in your prayer journal.
» Pray that God will help you apply what you are reading.

Day 3

» Continue to pray about your testimony and edit your original version of it.
» Read Acts 3 and Proverbs 3.
» Write in your prayer journal.
» Pray that God will help you apply what you are reading.

Day 4

» Continue to pray about your testimony and edit your original.
» Read Acts 4 and Proverbs 4.
» Write in your prayer journal.
» Pray that God will help you apply what you are reading.

Day 5

» Continue to pray about your testimony and edit your original.
» Read Acts 5 and Proverbs 5.
» Write in your prayer journal.
» Pray that God will help you apply what you are reading.

Day 6

» Continue to pray about your testimony; write the final draft of your testimony; remember to have a two minute, a ten minute, and a forty-five minute version of your testimony ready at all times.

» Read Acts 6 and Proverbs 6.

» Write in your prayer journal.

» Pray that God will help you apply what you are reading.

Days 7–10—MARRIAGE

Challenge: Love your wife as Christ loved the church. Be selfless. Do something for her for the next four days without expecting anything in return. (It takes only three days to start a habit.)

Day 7

» Pray that God will show you how a real man loves his wife.

» Read Acts 7, Ephesians 5, Colossians 3:18–25, and Proverbs 7.

» Write in your prayer journal.

» Do an act of selflessness for her today (wash dishes, clean something, spend time with her). Note: whatever you do, make it something you don't normally do—and do it for her, not to get points.

Day 8

» Pray that God will show you how a real man loves his wife.

» Read Acts 8, Ephesians 5, 1 Peter 3:7, and Proverbs 8.

» Write in your prayer journal.

> » Do another selfless act for your wife today. And not the same one that you did yesterday.

Day 9

> » Pray that God will show you how a real man loves his wife.
> » Read Acts 9, Ephesians 5, and Proverbs 9.
> » Write in your prayer journal.
> » Do another selfless act for your wife today. Something different.

Day 10

> » Pray that God will show you how a real man loves his wife.
> » Read Acts 10, Ephesians 5, and Proverbs 10.
> » Write in your prayer journal.
> » Do another selfless act for your wife today.
> » But don't stop after today. Keep loving her and doing things for her. You might be surprised about what you get out of doing these selfless acts. Remember, you start first.

Days 11–14—FATHERHOOD

Challenge: Turn off the TV, stop working, and spend time with your kids. Quality and quantity. Your kids deserve and need your time. In the next four days spend time with them doing what they want to do. But also keep in mind what Moses said in Deuteronomy 6:7–9.

Day 11

> » Pray that God will show you how to be a good father, a father whose children love and respect him.
> » Read Acts 11 and Proverbs 11.

» Write in your prayer journal.

» Turn off the TV, stop working, and just be with them, doing things they like (real men play dollhouse with their little girls).

Day 12

» Pray that God will show you how to be a good father, a father whose children love and respect him.

» Read Acts 12 and Proverbs 12.

» Write in your prayer journal.

» Turn off the TV, stop working, and just be with them, and do something fun with them that you don't normally do at a time you don't normally do it.

Day 13

» Pray that God will show you how to be a good father, a father whose children love and respect him.

» Read Acts 13 and Proverbs 13.

» Write in your prayer journal.

» Turn off the TV, stop working, and just be with them. Sit and talk with them about them and what they like to do and don't do.

Day 14

» Pray that God will show you how to be a good father, a father whose children love and respect him.

» Read Acts 14 and Proverbs 14.

» Write in your prayer journal.

» Turn off the TV, stop working, and just be with them. Read the Bible to them. Just read, and try to answer any questions they might have.

» Schedule a date night with your kids.

Almost halfway done, but this is just the beginning. Keep working on your testimony. Keep being selfless to your wife. Keep being the dad your kids need you to be. Stop with all of the outside stuff. If this means taking your kids out of sports or piano, then take them out, and spend more time with them.

One of your main jobs as a father is to protect your children. They don't know when to stop with all of the outside activities, but you should. So be the father they need, and just spend time with them. It's not quality over quantity—it's both quality and quantity.

Days 15–18—CHURCH

Challenge: Get involved at church. Pray over your spiritual gifts, and talk with your pastor or other church leaders. Then put your gifts into practice. Spend the next four days finding a place to fit into your church.

Day 15

- » Pray that God will show you how you can get involved in the church.
- » Read Acts 15 and Proverbs 15.
- » Take a spiritual gifts test if you haven't already.
- » Talk to your pastor or other church leaders about what is needed in the church.

Day 16

- » Pray that God will grant you the courage to step out and do what He has shown you.
- » Read Acts 16 and Proverbs 16.
- » Continue to seeks ways to get involved at church, and do something at church that no one will see

(e.g., vacuum the church, pray for your leaders before service, etc.).

Day 17

> » Pray that God will give you what you need for your church.
> » Read Acts 17 and Proverbs 17.
> » Get involved.

Day 18

> » Pray that God will give you what you need for your church.
> » Read Acts 18 and Proverbs 18.
> » Get involved.

After Day 18 you should still be working on your testimony. You should still be loving your wife and giving her more of you. You should still be spending time with your children. Now, continue to work in the church.

If you have not found a place to serve, you are not looking hard enough. Maybe you could visit people who aren't able to come to church because they are sick. Ask a new member over for lunch. Ask an older member over for lunch. Take the pastor to lunch and encourage him.

Days 19–22—WORK

Challenge: Live out the gospel at work. Take the next four days and be prepared for living out the gospel at work. Be prayed up and read up so you can stay up.

Day 19

> » Pray that God will use you at work. (He will, so be ready.)

» Read Acts 19 and Proverbs 19.
» Intentionally look for ways to share your faith and your testimony.
» Seek one person whom you would really like to get to know and share life with.

Day 20
» Pray that God will use you at work.
» Read Acts 20 and Proverbs 20.
» Intentionally look for ways to share your faith and your testimony.
» Seek one person whom you would really like to get to know and share life with.

Day 21
» Pray that God will use you at work.
» Read Acts 21 and Proverbs 21.
» Intentionally look for ways to share your faith and your testimony.
» Seek one person whom you would really like to get to know and share life with.

Day 22
» Pray that God will use you at work.
» Read Acts 22 and Proverbs 22.
» Intentionally look for ways to share your faith and your testimony.
» Seek one person whom you would really like to get to know and share life with.

It has been 22 days. You should still be using and revising your testimony. Remember, your testimony is just your story of how God has worked in your life. Big statement here: *You should still be performing selfless acts for your wife.* Don't stop doing that. You should still be looking for ways to spend time with your kids and with your wife. What are you doing in the church? You should be applying the Word more now to your life than you were ten days ago or even five days ago.

And keep looking for that one person to share life with. Or maybe it's more than one person. Look for the person to disciple or to be accountable with.

Days 23–26—ACCOUNTABILITY

Challenge: Pray for guidance to find an accountability partner. Find someone to share life with. You may even have had someone in mind already. Go talk to him.

Day 23

- » Pray for God to put a person in your life with whom you can be open and share your life.
- » Read Acts 23 and Proverbs 23.
- » Make a list of five people whom you think could be possible partners for accountability.
- » Pray over your list. Visit with these people over the next four to seven days.

Day 24

- » Pray for God to put a person in your life with whom you can be open and share your life.
- » Read Acts 24 and Proverbs 24.
- » Review your list and visit these men.
- » Pray over your list.

Day 25

- » Pray for God to put a person in your life with whom you can be open and share your life.

> » Read Acts 25 and Proverbs 25.
> » Review your list and visit these men.
> » Pray over your list.

Day 26

> » Pray for God to put a person in your life with whom you can be open and share your life.
> » Read Acts 26 and Proverbs 26.
> » Review your list and visit these men.
> » Pray over your list.

Note: If you haven't found someone by now, keep praying and keep looking. *Don't stop.* Also, if you haven't found someone at work to tell your testimony to, keep looking and praying.

Are you still trying to find ways to be selfless toward your wife? Are you still spending both quality time and quantity time with your kids? Are you serving in the church? Are you living out your testimony at work? Are you making the gospel look attractive with your actions? Have you found someone to be accountable to?

Days 27-30—DISCIPLESHIP

Challenge: Disciple or be discipled. If you have been discipled, then go find someone to impart the truth to. If you have not been discipled, go find someone to impart the truth to you.

Note: Do you need to be discipled? To find out, just answer this question: Have you been discipled? If you have been, then it's your turn to disciple. Find someone to take under your wing. If you have not been discipled, then you need to be. Find someone to disciple you. If you are not sure, then start by finding someone to disciple you.

Day 27

- » Pray that God will show you someone who will disciple you (or someone whom you can disciple).
- » Read Acts 27 and Proverbs 27. Make a list of men who you think could/would disciple you (or whom you could disciple).
- » Pray over that list and go talk with them about discipleship.

Day 28

- » Pray that God will show you someone who will disciple you (or someone whom you can disciple).
- » Read Acts 28 and Proverbs 28.
- » Make a list of men who you think could/would disciple you (or whom you could disciple).
- » Pray over that list and go talk with them about discipleship.

Day 29

- » Pray over your list and ask God to narrow it down.
- » Read your favorite part of Acts and/or Proverbs 24, and write out a handful of study questions for it.
- » Review your list and talk with those on the list.

Day 30

- » Pray that God will show you the exact person with whom He wants you to share your life.
- » Read Proverbs 30–31.
- » Review your list and talk with those on the list.

Your thirty days are up, and you have finished the challenge. If you have honestly taken this challenge then you should be a changed man. You have accepted the challenge to *Man Up!*

Your wife, your children, and those in your sphere of influence should have seen a difference. Don't stop doing your devotions, and now consider doing a family devotion. You can purchase a *Man Up! Family Devotion* at our website (manupgodsway.org). Take your family on a thirty day walk with Jesus.

My prayer is that you know that you know that Jesus died for your sins and that you are being transformed into His likeness every day. Also, I pray that you love your wife as Christ loved the church. I pray that you are spending more time with your children. I pray that you are involved in church and that your life is reflective of the gospel everywhere you go. I pray that you have men in your life whom you are accountable to—and other men whom you are discipling.

My friend, take these small things and make them big in your life. Share them with your sons and daughters, your friends, and other men who are what you used to be. My prayer is that you will take these small things and use them for the Glory of God.

In the name of Jesus Christ,
Amen

Accountability Covenant

1. Total and complete confidentiality.

What I hear here, see here, and say here stays here. I will say nothing to anyone that may be traced back or that could be injurious or embarrassing to my accountability partner.

2. Be as open as you can with your life.

I will be as open as I can with my life at this time. I will show myself to you, letting you know who I am as a person.

3. Unconditional love.

I will love you and affirm you no matter what you have said or done in the past. I will love you as you are and for what Christ wants to make of you.

4. Voluntary accountability.

I will ask you to hold me accountable for specific areas of my life. I give you my permission to ask me about the goals I set with God, my family, my personal life, and the world. I expect you to lovingly not "let me off the hook." "As iron sharpens iron, so one man sharpens another" (Proverbs 27:17). On the basis of this verse, I ask you to please share with me areas in my life that do not reflect Jesus, because I want to grow in personal holiness.

5. Pray for one another.

I promise to pray for you, my accountability partner, on a regular basis, to lift up your needs to the Lord.

6. Come prepared each week.

I will have my work completed and my verse memorized each week when I come to our meeting. I will make every effort to be at our meeting. It will have high priority in my schedule.

Signed: _____

Signed: _____

How To Study the Bible

1. Pray. (Always begin your study by praying. Ask God to reveal His truth to you and give you understanding.)
2. Choose what to read. (Start with a book of the Bible. Try not to jump around. Pick a book and finish it.)
3. Observations. As you read answer these questions:

   » Who? Who is speaking, who wrote the book or passage, who is listening, and who is around (in the crowd)?
   » What? What is going on around them? What is the time of the day and year? What is being said? And what is the reaction to what is said?
   » Where? Location? Where are the events taking place?
   » Why? Are there people together? Are people reacting to what is said?

4. Interpretation:

   » Content—Who, what, where, and why (together)?
   » Context—What is being said or done before and after this passage?
   » Compare—With other Scripture (use cross references).

5. Application:

>> Relate—How does this relate to my life, someone else's life, to life in general?
>> Meditate—Day and night; pray on it; let it consume you.
>> Practice—Put it into practice.

Questions to Ask:

1. Is there an example here for me to follow?
2. Is there any sin the Lord wants me to avoid or repent of?
3. Is there a promise for me to claim?
4. Is there a prayer for me to repeat?
5. Is there a command to obey?

Resources:

1. Biblegateway.com (here you can read in different translations quickly)
2. Blueletterbible.org (commentary, word search, definitions)
3. Desiringgod.org (sermons, articles, and blog from John Piper)
4. Gty.org (sermons, articles, and blog from John MacArthur)
5. sovereigngraceministries.org (sermons, articles, and blog from C.J. Mahaney)
6. christiananswers.net/dictionary/home.html (names, places, and foods of the Bible)

Notes:

1. Pray, pray, pray.
2. Pray for God to reveal His truths (not for you to prove a point or read something into it that is not there).
3. Make the time to study, not just to read Scripture.
4. Read the passage and write down questions. (Come back later to answer questions.)
5. Find someone to study with or to talk to about what you are studying.

READ THE BIBLE THROUGH IN ONE YEAR IN CHRONOLOGICAL ORDER

JANUARY

1 Genesis 1–3
2 Genesis 4–7
3 Genesis 8–11
4 Job 1–5
5 Job 6–9
6 Job 10–13
7 Job 14–16
8 Job 17–20
9 Job 21–23
10 Job 24–28
11 Job 29–31
12 Job 32–34
13 Job 35–37
14 Job 38–39
15 Job 40–42
16 Genesis 12–15
17 Genesis 16–18
18 Genesis 19–21
19 Genesis 22–24
20 Genesis 25–26
21 Genesis 27–29
22 Genesis 30–31
23 Genesis 32–34
24 Genesis 35–37
25 Genesis 38–40
26 Genesis 41–42
27 Genesis 43–45
28 Genesis 46–47
29 Genesis 48–50
30 Exodus 1–3
31 Exodus 4–6

FEBRUARY

1 Exodus 7–9
2 Exodus 10–12
3 Exodus 13–15
4 Exodus 16–18
5 Exodus 19–21
6 Exodus 22–24
7 Exodus 25–27
8 Exodus 28–29
9 Exodus 30–32
10 Exodus 33–35
11 Exodus 36–38
12 Exodus 39–40
13 Leviticus 1–4
14 Leviticus 5–7
15 Leviticus 8–10
16 Leviticus 11–13
17 Leviticus 14–15
18 Leviticus 16–18
19 Leviticus 19–21
20 Leviticus 22–23
21 Leviticus 24–25
22 Leviticus 26–27

23 Numbers 1–2
24 Numbers 3–4
25 Numbers 5–6
26 Numbers 7
27 Numbers 8–10
28 Numbers 11–13

MARCH
1 Numbers 14–15; Psalms 90
2 Numbers 16–17
3 Numbers 18–20
4 Numbers 21–22
5 Numbers 23–25
6 Numbers 26–27
7 Numbers 28–30
8 Numbers 31–32
9 Numbers 33–34
10 Numbers 35–36
11 Deuteronomy 1–2
12 Deuteronomy 3–4
13 Deuteronomy 5–7
14 Deuteronomy 8–10
15 Deuteronomy 11–13
16 Deuteronomy 14–16
17 Deuteronomy 17–20
18 Deuteronomy 21–23
19 Deuteronomy 24–27
20 Deuteronomy 28–29
21 Deuteronomy 30–31
22 Deuteronomy 32–34;
   Psalms 91

23 Joshua 1–4
24 Joshua 5–8
25 Joshua 9–11
26 Joshua 12–15
27 Joshua 16–18
28 Joshua 19–21
29 Joshua 22–24
30 Judges 1–2
31 Judges 3–5

APRIL
1 Judges 6–7
2 Judges 8–9
3 Judges 10–12
4 Judges 13–15
5 Judges 16–18
6 Judges 19–21
7 Ruth
8 1 Samuel 1–3
9 1 Samuel 4–8
10 1 Samuel 9–12
11 1 Samuel 13–14
12 1 Samuel 15–17
13 1 Samuel 18–20; Psalms
   11; Psalms 59
14 1 Samuel 21–24
15 Psalms 7; 27; 31; 34; 52
16 Psalms 56; 120;140–142
17 1 Samuel 25–27
18 Psalms 17; 35; 54; 63
19 1 Samuel 28–31; Psalms18

20 Psalm 121;
123–125;128–130
21 2 Samuel 1–4
22 Psalms 6; 8–10; 14; 16;
19; 21
23 1 Chronicles 1–2
24 Psalms 43–45; 49; 84–85;
87
25 1 Chronicles 3–5
26 Psalms 73; 77–78
27 1 Chronicles 6
28 Psalms 81; 88; 92–93
29 1 Chronicles 7–10 30
Psalms 102–104

MAY

1 2 Samuel 5:1–10;
1 Chronicles 11–12
2 Psalms 133
3 Psalms 106–107
4 2 Samuel 5:11–6:23; 1
Chronicles 13–16
5 Psalms 1–2; 15; 22–24; 47;
68
6 Psalms 89; 96; 100; 101;
105; 132
7 2 Samuel 7; 1 Chronicles
17
8 Psalms 25; 29; 33; 36; 39
9 2 Samuel 8–9; 1 Chronicles
18

10 Psalms 50; 53; 60; 75
11 2 Samuel 10; 1 Chronicles
19;
Psalms 20
12 Psalms 65–67; 69–70
13 2 Samuel 11–12; 1
Chronicles 20
14 Psalms 32; 51; 86; 122
15 2 Samuel 13–15
16 Psalms 3–4; 12–13; 28;
55
17 2 Samuel 16–18
18 Psalms 26; 40; 58; 61–62;
64
19 2 Samuel 19–21
20 Psalms 5; 38; 41–42
21 2 Samuel 22–23; Psalms
57
22 Psalms 95; 97–99
23 2 Samuel 24; 1 Chronicles
21–22;
Psalms 30
24 Psalms 108–110
25 1 Chronicles 23–25
26 Psalms 131; 138–139;
143–145
27 1 Chronicles 26–29;
Psalms 127
28 Psalms 111–118
29 1 Kings 1–2; Psalms 37;
71; 94

30 Psalms 119:1–88
31 1 Kings 3–4; 2 Chronicles 1; Psalms 72

JUNE

1 Psalms 119:89–176
2 Song of Solomon
3 Proverbs 1–3
4 Proverbs 4–6
5 Proverbs 7–9
6 Proverbs 10–12
7 Proverbs 13–15
8 Proverbs 16–18
9 Proverbs 19–21
10 Proverbs 22–24
11 1 Kings 5–6; 2 Chronicles 2–3
12 1 Kings 7; 2 Chronicles 4
13 1 Kings 8; 2 Chronicles 5
14 2 Chronicles 6–7; Psalms 136
15 Psalms 134; 146–150
16 1 Kings 9; 2 Chronicles 8
17 Proverbs 25–26
18 Proverbs 27–29
19 Ecclesiastes 1–6
20 Ecclesiastes 7–12
21 1 Kings 10–11; 2 Chronicles 9
22 Proverbs 30–31
23 1 Kings 12–14

24 2 Chronicles 10–12
25 1 Kings 15:1–24; 2 Chronicles 13–16
26 1 Kings 15:25–16:34; 2 Chronicles 17
27 1 Kings 17–19
28 1 Kings 20–21
29 1 Kings 22; 2 Chronicles 18
30 2 Chronicles 19–23

JULY

1 Obadiah; Psalms 82–83
2 2 Kings 1–4
3 2 Kings 5–8
4 2 Kings 9–11
5 2 Kings 12–13 ; 2 Chronicles 24
6 2 Kings 14; 2 Chronicles 25
7 Jonah
8 2 Kings 15; 2 Chronicles 26
9 Isaiah 1–4
10 Isaiah 5–8
11 Amos 1–5
12 Amos 6–9
13 2 Chronicles 27; Isaiah 9–12
14 Micah
15 2 Chronicles 28; 2 Kings

16–17
16 Isaiah 13–17
17 Isaiah 18–22
18 Isaiah 23–27
19 2 Kings 18:1–8; 2
Chronicles 29–31;
Psalms 48
20 Hosea 1–7
21 Hosea 8–14
22 Isaiah 28–30
23 Isaiah 31–34
24 Isaiah 35–36
25 Isaiah 37–39; Psalms 76
26 Isaiah 40–43
27 Isaiah 44–48
28 2 Kings 18:9–19:37;
Psalms 46; 80;135
29 Isaiah 49–53
30 Isaiah 54–58
31 Isaiah 59–63

AUGUST
1 Isaiah 64–66
2 2 Kings 20–21
3 2 Chronicles 32–33
4 Nahum
5 2 Kings 22–23;
2 Chronicles 34–35
6 Zephaniah
7 Jeremiah 1–3
8 Jeremiah 4–6

9 Jeremiah 7–9
10 Jeremiah 10–13
11 Jeremiah 14–17
12 Jeremiah 18–22
13 Jeremiah 23–25
14 Jeremiah 26–29
15 Jeremiah 30–31
16 Jeremiah 32–34
17 Jeremiah 35–37
18 Jeremiah 38–40; Psalms
74; 79
19 2 Kings 24–25; 2
Chronicles 36
20 Habakkuk
21 Jeremiah 41–45
22 Jeremiah 46–48
23 Jeremiah 49–50
24 Jeremiah 51–52
25 Lamentations 1:1–3:36
26 Lamentations 3:37–5:22
27 Ezekiel 1–4
28 Ezekiel 5–8
29 Ezekiel 9–12
30 Ezekiel 13–15
31 Ezekiel 16–17

SEPTEMBER
1 Ezekiel 18–19
2 Ezekiel 20–21
3 Ezekiel 22–23
4 Ezekiel 24–27

5 Ezekiel 28–31
6 Ezekiel 32–34
7 Ezekiel 35–37
8 Ezekiel 38–39
9 Ezekiel 40–41
10 Ezekiel 42–43
11 Ezekiel 44–45
12 Ezekiel 46–48
13 Joel
14 Daniel 1–3
15 Daniel 4–6
16 Daniel 7–9
17 Daniel 10–12
18 Ezra 1–3
19 Ezra 4–6; Psalms 137
20 Haggai
21 Zechariah 1–7
22 Zechariah 8–14
23 Esther 1–5
24 Esther 6–10
25 Ezra 7–10
26 Nehemiah 1–5
27 Nehemiah 6–7
28 Nehemiah 8–10
29 Nehemiah 11–13; Psalms 126
30 Malachi

OCTOBER

1 Luke 1 ; John 1:1–14
2 Matthew 1; Luke 2:1–38
3 Matthew 2; Luke 2:39–52
4 Matthew 3; Mark 1; Luke 3
5 Matthew 4; Luke 4–5; John 1:15–51
6 John 2–4
7 Mark 2
8 John 5
9 Matthew 12:1–21; Mark 3; Luke 6
10 Matthew 5–7
11 Matthew 8:1–13; Luke 7
12 Matthew 11
13 Matthew 12:22–50; Luke 11
14 Matthew 13; Luke 8
15 Matthew 8:14–34; Mark 4–5
16 Matthew 9–10
17 Matthew 14; Mark 6; Luke 9:1–17
18 John 6
19 Matthew 15; Mark 7
20 Matthew 16; Mark 8; Luke 9:18–27
21 Matthew 17; Mark 9; Luke 9:28–62
22 Matthew 18
23 John 7–8
24 John 9:1–10:21
25 Luke 10–11; John

10:22–42
26 Luke 12–13
27 Luke 14–15
28 Luke 16–17:10
29 John 11
30 Luke 17:11–18:14
31 Matthew 19; Mark 10

NOVEMBER
1 Matthew 20–21
2 Luke 18:15–19:48
3 Mark 11; John 12
4 Matthew 22; Mark 12
5 Matthew 23; Luke 20–21
6 Mark 13
7 Matthew 24
8 Matthew 25
9 Matthew 26; Mark 14
10 Luke 22; John 13
11 John 14–17
12 Matthew 27; Mark 15
13 Luke 23; John 18–19
14 Matthew 28; Mark 16
15 Luke 24; John 20–21
16 Acts 1–3
17 Acts 4–6
18 Acts 7–8
19 Acts 9–10
20 Acts 11–12
21 Acts 13–14
22 James

23 Acts 15–16
24 Galatians 1–3
25 Galatians 4–6
26 Acts 17–18:18
27 1 Thessalonians; 2 Thessalonians
28 Acts 18:19–19:41
29 1 Corinthians 1–4
30 1 Corinthians 5–8

DECEMBER
1 1 Corinthians 9–11
2 1 Corinthians 12–14
3 1 Corinthians 15–16
4 2 Corinthians 1–4
5 2 Corinthians 5–9
6 2 Corinthians 10–13
7 Acts 20:1–3; Romans 1–3
8 Romans 4–7
9 Romans 8–10
10 Romans 11–13
11 Romans 14–16
12 Acts 20:4–23:35
13 Acts 24–26
14 Acts 27–28
15 Colossians; Philemon
16 Ephesians
17 Philippians
18 1 Timothy
19 Titus
20 1 Peter

Jody,

1/27/99

How are you Brother? Last time we talked on the phone, I told you I had something for you. I recently attended a program keepers and you & Nan were on my mind. I don't want to come off like a religious freak or anything but it was a powerful gathering and if there was anyone in the world that I would wanted to share this with it was you. I picked up this bible for you because I felt moved to and I would like to invite you to go with me to promise keepers next year. Notice I'm giving you some time to think about it. Anyway I wanted you to have this because we are all down here struggling & searching, well of course I'm late 😊 I'll close for now.

Take care,

Endnotes

Chapter 4

[1] *U.S. Congregational Life Survey – Key Findings,* 29 October 2003, <www.uscongregations.org/key.htm>.

[2] This statistic comes from Barna's figures on male/female worship attendance, overlaid upon the Census 2000 numbers for adult men and women in the U.S. population.

[3] I came up with this figure by taking the U.S. Census 2000 numbers for total married adults and overlaying Barna Research's year 2000 percentages of male vs. female attendance at weekly worship services. The figures suggest at least 24.5 million married women attend church on a given weekend, but only 19 million married men attend. That's 5.5 million more women or 22.5%. The actual number may be even higher, because married people attend church in much greater numbers than singles.

[4] *Barna Research Online,* "Women are the Backbone of Christian Congregations in America," 6 March 2000, <www.barna. org>.

[5] Ibid.

[6] "LifeWay Research Uncovers Reasons 18 to 22 Year Olds Drop Out of Church," PowerPoint presentation accompanying study, available at the LifeWay Web site, http://www.lifeway. com/lwc/article_main_page/0,1703,A=165949&M=200906, 00.html, accessed 12 September 2007.

[7] Barna, "Women are the Backbone of Christian Congregations in America."

[8] I get an e-mail message about once a month from a pastor overseas whose congregation is almost totally female.

[9] Camerin Courtney, "O Brother, Where Art Thou?" Christianity Today, Single Minded. View at http://www.christianitytoday.com/singles/newsletter/mind40630.html.

[10] Based on a show of hands at the National Coalition of Men's Ministries meeting in 2005. The consensus in the room among hundreds of men's ministry experts was that less than 10% of congregations had any ongoing ministry to men. Compare this to the 110% of churches that offer women's and children's ministries.

[11, 12] "Why Religion Matters: The Impact of Religious Practice on Social Stability," *The Heritage Foundation Backgrounder,* 1064, 25 January 1996, <www.heritage.org>.

[13] Penny Edgell (Becker) and Heather Hofmeister, "Work, Family and Religious Involvement for Men and Women," *Hartford Institute for Religion Research,* <http://hirr.hartsem.edu>.

[14] Christian Smith and Phillip Kim, "Religious Youth Are More Likely to Have Positive Relationships with Their Fathers," University of North Carolina at Chapel Hill, 12 July 2002, findings based on the *National Longitudinal Survey of Youth* (1997).

[15] C. Kirk Hadaway, FACTs on Growth: A New Look at the Dynamics of Growth and Decline in American Congregations Based on the Faith Communities Today. *2005 national survey of Congregations.* Hartford Institute for Religion Research, http://hirr.hartsem.edu.

Chapter 5

[1] Source: www.cdc.gov/nchs/data/hus/hus07.pdf.